(1ST U.S. ed., 1983) (O.p.) 12 -

LA. 7 50

CHANDLERTOWN

By the same author

The Night I Caught the Santa Fe Chief

CHANDLERTOWN
The Los Angeles of Philip Marlowe

Edward Thorpe

St. Martin's Press
New York

Library of Congress Cataloging in Publication Data

Thorpe, Edward.
    Chandlertown: the Los Angeles of Philip Marlowe.

    1. Chandler, Raymond, 1888-1959—Settings.
2. Los Angeles (Calif.)—Description. 3. Chandler,
Raymond, 1888-1959—Characters—Philip Marlowe.
I. Title.
PS3505.H3224Z87 1984   813'.52   83-24413
ISBN 0-312-12851-7

First Published in Great Britain in 1983 by Vermilion & Company

First U.S. Edition

10 9 8 7 6 5 4 3 2 1

CONTENTS

For
Arlen and Shel Stuart

AUTHOR'S NOTE

A great deal of Raymond Chandler's Los Angeles, which he documented so accurately in his novels and short stories, still remains visible among the new high-rise buildings of Hollywood and the apartment blocks of 'Bay City' (Santa Monica). The photographs were taken in the late seventies and early eighties and show how the Art-Deco department stores, the Hollywood office blocks, the cheap waterfront dives which were Marlowe's milieu, are still an essential visual element of Chandlertown.

The author wishes to thank Mrs. Helga Greene for permission to quote from the works of Raymond Chandler.

Except where indicated, all the photographs are by the author.

1
ALL COLOURS OF THE SPECTRUM

Los Angeles was Raymond Chandler's town; Philip Marlowe's town too. No other fictional detective has been so identified, so involved with the environment of a particular city as Marlowe is with Los Angeles – except perhaps Sherlock Holmes with London or Maigret with Paris.

Marlowe's activities were concentrated between 1939 and 1958, years in which the outline of the contemporary megalopolis began to be superimposed on the townships, settlements, rancheros and plantations that had been developed in the Los Angeles basin during the two hundred years since the Spanish colonists first began to dispossess the native Indian tribes who lived there. But we are only concerned here with two decades out of those two centuries, years during which, as in so many fast-growing cities of the United States, crime and corruption were part of the social fabric attendant upon rapid commercial development.

The areas that Marlowe knew and ranged so explicitly in Chandler's fiction – downtown Los Angeles itself, Hollywood, Beverly Hills, Bel Air, Westwood, Brentwood – are still there, distinct, with their own especial ambience, visual styles and psychological climates which Chandler recorded so lovingly and accurately as the background for his world-weary, cynical hero.

Filling his pipe, making his coffee with care, looking out of his office or his apartment window as dusk fell on the sprawling city, musing on the crimes that were being committed out of greed and passion, Marlowe was often weary of human folly and evil. But never weary of the city itself, Marlowe frequently expressed his divided attitude towards it:

> Past all this and down a wide smooth curve to the bridle path of Beverly Hills and lights to the south, all colours of the spectrum and crystal clear in an evening without fog, past the mansions up on the hills to the north, past Beverly Hills altogether and up into the twisting Foothills Boulevard and the sudden cool dusk and the drift of wind from the sea. (*Farewell, My Lovely*)

11

Or:

> I smelled Los Angeles before I got to it. It smelled stale and old like a living room that had been closed too long. But the coloured lights fooled you. The lights were wonderful. (*The Little Sister*)

Chandler's Marlowe knew Los Angeles in every mood: hot and smoggy, the air heavy with carbon monoxide and the suggestion of the smell of blood, or deceptively fresh, washed with rain, scented with chaparral and corruption. Always there is an overlay of deception and decay, a beautiful location blighted by man, a perfect night marred by murder. Mean streets and magnificent mansions, waterfront bars and suburban cocktail lounges, Marlowe knew them all as he crossed and recrossed Chandlertown, a private eye whose restlessness in a restless city not only records, incidentally, the social and geographical growth of a great metropolis but provides an exciting, atmospheric *mise-en-scène* for his adventures on paper and celluloid.

It is precisely this constant movement, this opening out, that makes Chandler's fiction, especially the Marlowe stories, not only fast-paced on the page but also such natural movie material. And it is the exact use of locale, the naming of streets and shops, the descriptions of smells and sights and sounds readily identifiable with a specific area that makes Greater Los Angeles almost as important a character as Marlowe himself. It is the sociogeographical uniqueness of the city, its amazing amalgam of grotesque film-industry extravaganza, of the respectable middle-class suburbs, of the big-time racketeers and small-time crooks, its subtropical climate, its mountains and beaches and surrounding desert, that provides such an endlessly fascinating background for Marlowe. Put him in any other big city, however romantic – New York, Chicago, San Francisco, New Orleans – and he might be just another down-at-heel dick grubbing a livelihood from the pickings of a metropolitan muck heap like so many of his imitators.

Raymond Chandler portrayed Los Angeles with an accuracy that was sometimes affectionate and sometimes cruel. Nowadays his Marlowe adventures have the added attraction of nostalgia – the Art-Deco architecture and decor, the Chrysler sedans and Packard coupés. Either way the stories and the city stand up to cinematic exploration: Robert Altman's contemporary version of *The Long Goodbye*, Dick Richards's period remake of *Farewell, My Lovely*. Both cities – Richards's original and Altman's contemporary – exist, compellingly, side by side. The main visual features of Los Angeles's amazing growth are the great clusters of high-rise buildings and the vast network of freeways. In between are the diverse districts and individual setpieces that Marlowe would instantly recognize.

2
A WORLD GONE WRONG

Raymond Chandler was born on 23 July 1888, in Chicago, Illinois. His mother, Florence Dart Thornton, was Irish, his father, Maurice Benjamin Chandler, American. When Raymond was eight years old his parents were divorced, and Florence brought her small son to England, sending him as a day boy to Dulwich College where, among his contemporaries were P.G. Wodehouse and Boris Karloff. He remained there until the age of seventeen, then spent a year in France and Germany, which appears to have made no lasting impact. Continental Europe did not spark his creative imagination and had little significant influence on his work: the social mores and architectural styles, progenitors of ethnic American behaviour, eating habits and homesteads, fascinated him only in their transmuted forms, second hand as it were, when absorbed into the American way of life. There always remained, however, a respect, if not an affection, for the formative English modes and manners (most apparent in the limited collection of published correspondence*), and throughout the novels recognizable upper-class British stereotypes make their mark, based on his adolescent memories carried over into adult awareness.

On his return to England in 1907 he studied for the civil service and entered the Admiralty, where he worked for only six months. From then on, living in Bloomsbury, he worked as a freelance journalist for the *Academy*, the *Westminster Gazette* and the *Spectator*. In 1912 he went back to the United States, moving to California, which was to become the most positive influence on his work and life. At the outbreak of the First World War he enlisted in the Canadian army, serving in France. In 1918 Chandler transferred to the RFC and in 1919, when he was demobilized, he returned again to California, this time with his mother. He took various jobs – on an apricot ranch, stringing tennis rackets – then taught himself book-keeping. Thus he entered the

---

**Raymond Chandler Speaking*, edited by Dorothy Gardiner and Kathrine Sorley Walker (Hamish Hamilton, 1962).

business world, eventually becoming a director of a number of oil companies, work eventually terminated by the depression.

His mother died in 1924 and shortly afterwards Chandler married Pearl Cecily (Cissy) Bowen. She was seventeen years older than he and twice divorced, but it was a marriage of enduring devotion. In the early thirties and out of work, 'wandering up and down the Pacific coast', Chandler began reading pulp magazine stories and found them 'forceful and honest'. He had always wanted to be a writer and thought that writing for such publications would be a good way to learn the techniques for such fiction while earning a little money at the same time.

His first effort was an 18,000 word novelette, 'Blackmailers Don't Shoot', published in *Black Mask*, for which he was paid $180. After that, he said, he 'never looked back'. For six years he wrote stories for detective magazines (*Black Mask, Detective Fiction Weekly, Dime Detective Magazine*) then, in 1939, he published his first full-length novel, *The Big Sleep*,* which established him as a major crime novelist.

Other works followed in fairly quick succession with *Farewell, My Lovely* in 1940, *The High Window* and *The Lady in the Lake* in 1943, together with half a dozen short stories in magazines, some of which were later partly reworked into his novels. 'The Lady in the Lake', published in *Dime Detective Magazine* in 1939 was one of these.

In 1943 Chandler, already very middle-aged at fifty-five, went to Hollywood. The previous year *Farewell, My Lovely* had made its first film appearance as the basis for the RKO Radio picture, *The Falcon Takes Over*. He was to adapt his own work as well as writing original screenplays. For Paramount he wrote *Double Indemnity* in collaboration with Billy Wilder, *And Now Tomorrow* with Frank Partos and *The Unseen* with Hagar Wilde. *Farewell, My Lovely* was used for a second time as the basis for a filmscript – titled *Murder My Sweet* (again for RKO), it takes its place in history as the vehicle for the first screen Philip Marlowe, amiably played by Dick Powell.

Three years later Raymond and Cissy Chandler moved a hundred miles down the coast to La Jolla. Cissy's health was poor. Chandler continued to write novels as well as screenplays. *The Blue Dahlia* (Paramount), *The Big Sleep* (Warner), *The High Window* retitled as *The Brasher Doubloon* (20th Century Fox), *The Lady in the Lake* (Metro-Goldwyn-Mayer) and, in collaboration with Patricia Highsmith, *Strangers on a Train* (Warner) were made between 1946 and 1950. *The Little Sister* was published in 1949 and *The Long Goodbye* in 1953. In 1954 Cissy died, leaving Chandler suicidal. He was not able to write for three years. His last complete novel, *Playback* and his last short story,

*Alfred A. Knopf (USA); Hamish Hamilton (UK).

The Pencil, were written in 1958.* In 1959 he began a new book, *The Poodle Springs Story*, but he died in La Jolla before finishing it.

Chandler was always self-conscious about his ability as a writer. Despite the then low status of his genre, he gave great consideration to plot construction, character development and prose style. He was particularly pleased when critics (and fans) thought of him as a writer rather than as a *crime* writer. Among his essays is a perceptive critique of the mystery novel and in his published letters there are many references, both from his own work and that of others, to the elements that constitute 'good' writing. Perhaps his major fictional achievement – the seven novels which feature Philip Marlowe, private investigator – is to have developed the mystery story from the stultified puzzle 'how did the murderer escape from the locked-room?' syndrome into works which utilize 'heightened reality'; 'real' characters in a real time and a real place.

To accomplish this, apart from following the classical formulas for any work of art – structure, shape, style – he made assiduous use of actual locations, characters and situations. Names were changed, streets or areas sometimes rejuxtaposed so as to avoid identification (and a possible libel suit!), but again and again while gathering material or researching some reference I found the real-life parallel to a fictional scenario.

In his letters, essays and critiques, Chandler makes little or no reference to Los Angeles itself, or to his obvious fascination with it as a perfect microcosm of man's estate. Yet his consistent use of the city and its environs in his fiction almost constitutes a sociopolitical history of America's largest conurbation, and reveals, through the eyes of Philip Marlowe, Chandler's acute sensitivity to the pulse of big-city life as a backdrop for misery and madness.

When I got home I mixed a stiff one and stood by the open window in the living room and sipped it and listened to the ground swell of the traffic on Laurel Canyon Boulevard and looked at the glare of the big, angry city hanging over the shoulder of the hills through which the boulevard had been cut. Far off the banshee wail of police or fire sirens rose and fell, never for very long completely silent. Twenty-four hours a day somebody is running, somebody else is trying to catch him. Out there in the night of a thousand crimes people were dying, being maimed, cut by flying glass, crushed against steering wheels or under heavy car tyres. People were being beaten, robbed, strangled, raped and murdered. People were hungry, sick, bored, desperate with loneliness or remorse or fear, angry, cruel, feverish, shaken by sobs. A city no worse than others, a city rich and vigorous and full of pride, a city lost and beaten and full of emptiness. (*The Long Goodbye*)

*'The Pencil' was first published posthumously in *Manhunt* (1960).

Not a flattering portrait of Los Angeles perhaps, but written in the context of Marlowe's perceptions in a depressed mood. And Chandler never forgot that it is the people, malicious, greedy, depraved, vengeful against society in general and each other in particular, who make any city what it is, give it a reputation for vice and venality. Throughout the novels runs an awareness of the natural beauties of the locale, the aromatic airs of the canyons heavy with the scent of night jasmin, juniper and eucalyptus, the grandeur of the surrounding mountains, the sweep of the coastline, the cooling winds from the sea, even the man-made carpet of lights stretching from the Hollywood Hills to the edge of the desert. Chandler used it all, observed accurately and dwelt deliberately on the mean and the magnificent in order to compose the visual mosaics that provide the settings for his mysteries.

The surprising – and, to the Chandlerphile, satisfying – aspect is that so much of Marlowe's Los Angeles remains to perpetuate the forties atmosphere. Dean Tavoularis, art director of the 1970s remake of *Farewell, My Lovely*, had little difficulty in finding locations, both interior and exterior, to create the period feel of the film.

Chandler's closely defined ambience of excitement and mystery, born of corruption and decadence, the manipulation of wealth and power, the danger attendant upon material success, still hovers like smog over the city. In the introduction to his collected short stories, Chandler wrote:

> Possibly it was the smell of fear which the stories managed to generate. Their characters lived in a world gone wrong, a world in which, long before the atom bomb, civilization had created the machinery for its own destruction, and was learning to use it with all the moronic delight of a gangster trying out his first machine gun. The law was something to be manipulated for profit and power. The streets were dark with something more than night.

It is Chandler's own précis of almost all he wrote, and the most significant phrase is surely 'The law was something to be manipulated for profit and power.' What more profitable and powerful city than Los Angeles? What greater profit than that wielded by the (then) major resident cinema industry, and what greater power, both in direct material wealth and in indirect influence, than the film factories themselves? Hollywood has much to answer for, besides providing work for, and a mirror image of, Philip Marlowe.

For Chandler the streets could be dark at noon, too. Whatever a film director or a lighting cameraman might prefer, he knew that the boulevards of Beverly Hills, the canyons of Bel Air, the waterfront dives of Bay City,* the sleazy streets of Hollywood itself could be just as

*Santa Monica. See chapter 5.

sinister, just as dangerous by day. Marlowe could discover a murder in a frowsy flop-house or be threatened by a beautiful blonde wielding an automatic in an elegant living room while Chandler illumined the details with the perennial Californian sunlight.

Whether or not today's casual visitor to Los Angeles will find himself in need of Marlowe's services depends very much on his own life style; he can certainly retrace Marlowe's footsteps around Chandlertown, receive very similar impressions and sensations, absorb the excitement, sense the danger, admire the beauty, resent the rackets, react to the perception of *déjà vu* provided so accurately by Chandler's literary portrait of Marlowe's milieu.

3

BECAUSE THEY ARE PHONEY

Marlowe's adventures usually bring him into contact with the rich. Sometimes they are the established upper class, sometimes the new rich who may or may not have come by their money legitimately. Either way, Marlowe views them with suspicion and cynicism. Sometimes he reveals a grudging admiration for the trappings of wealth, although often there is an acute awareness of the difference between expensive good taste and vulgar luxury.

Like his creator, Marlowe was something of a snob despite being a financial failure, which Chandler obviously was not, although he did not attain the super salaries of the Hollywood stars.

> I am ... by tradition and long study a complete snob. P. Marlowe and I do not despise the upper classes because they take baths and have money; we despise them because they are phoney. (*Raymond Chandler Speaking*)

Of course, much of Hollywood (and here it seems justifiable to use Hollywood as a synonym for Los Angeles) and its life style is almost essentially phoney. It is, after all, peddling make-believe as well as being concerned with maintaining its hierarchy of success through the traditional status symbols of affluence – big houses, flashy cars, jewels, furs, appearances at the right (i.e. fashionable) places – none of it possible without money and much of it a front.

To be without money in Hollywood – even in the eighties – is automatically to be branded as a failure, to be socially ostracized. It has always been so:

> If being in revolt against a corrupt society constitutes being immature, then Philip Marlowe is extremely immature. If seeing dirt where there is dirt constitutes an inadequate social adjustment then Philip Marlowe has inadequate social adjustment. Of course Marlowe is a failure and he knows it. He is a failure because he hasn't any money. (*Raymond Chandler Speaking*)

Those who do have money have always made it apparent with varying degrees of discretion. In Hollywood itself, in Beverly Hills, in Bel Air

18

and in the canyons running inland from the coast, most of the magnificent mansions proclaim the wealth of the owners with a vulgarity often manifested by every architectural caprice imaginable.

The Sternwood mansion, which is described in detail in the opening pages of *The Big Sleep*, was in Alta Brea, a fictitious street running up to the Hollywood Hills but one which is recognizable from several real-life houses. It is gloomy with stained glass and wrought iron, sinister with the associations of tropical flowers – fleshy, fungoid, requiring a steamy artificial atmosphere in which to live. The old, dying General Sternwood, surrounded by his orchids, is symptomatic of Chandler's feelings for a faded aristocracy, senile, impotent, ironically in need of Marlowe's health and virility – however impoverished he might be in monetary terms – to root out the canker in a wealthy but decadent family. Once again it is Chandler's familiar Los Angeles equation: rich equals degenerate, poor equals honest.

In another part of the house lives General Sternwood's eldest daughter, her own ostentatiously furnished apartments described in terms which once more equate luxury with a deathly pallor:

> The room was too big, the ceiling was too high, the doors were too tall and the white carpet that went from wall to wall was like a fresh fall of snow at Lake Arrowhead. There were full-length mirrors and crystal doodads all over the place. The ivory furniture had chromium on it and the enormous ivory drapes lay tumbled on the white carpet a yard from the windows. The white made the ivory look dirty and the ivory made the white look bled out.

'Dirty' and 'bled out' are, of course, the salient words in the description.

Whatever emotional and psychological overtones there are in Chandler's scene-setting, and in Marlowe's reaction to it, there is no doubt that Chandler had seen a number of rooms like that and could still do so today, in at least three variations: the real thing, still surviving; a deliberate recreation of the period style; and a contemporary interpretation of the all-white chromium theme – from the Bauhaus to Bel Air and back again.

This visual Chinese box of tricks, this psychological time slip aided and abetted by Hollywood's own manipulation of it, is something that constantly affects one in Chandlertown. A sudden view of a huge house perched on the side of a canyon, an imitation Art-Deco barroom, a forties car parked in a palm-fringed driveway, gives one an instant replay of last night's late-night movie.

Chandler's personal tastes in homes and furnishings can only be surmised from his novels and stories, and there is nothing explicit in his other writings, either. His literary descriptions, however, in as much as they are intended to reflect the tastes of his characters, are often

19

The Sternwood mansion, described in The Big Sleep, *is full of gothic motifs, but the Hollywood Hills, where the Sternwoods lived, is full of grand houses built in many styles of which this Southern Colonial mansion is typical. It was certainly there in Chandler's day, situated in the area around Franklin Avenue which Chandler describes several times*

Right: *In* Farewell My Lovely *Chandler refers to Beverly Hills as 'the best policed four square miles in California'. Today, as in the thirties, it includes some magnificent mansions belonging to Hollywood celebrities, as well as what are probably the world's most expensive and vulgarly ostentatious shopping streets. As this photograph shows, however, its Spanish-style City Hall retains its period splendour*

Pacific Palisades, adjacent to 'Bay City' (Santa Monica), is another residential area full of grand houses like the one in this photograph, many of them built in the twenties and thirties. In his early short story 'Pearls Are A Nuisance', Chandler remarks, somewhat acidly, 'Pacific Palisades is a district whose inhabitants seem to retire rather early'

elliptical indications of his approval or disapproval filtered to the reader through Marlowe's somewhat jaundiced eye.

Marlowe's rich clients usually have something to hide (the poor ones are more likely to be trying to get something back), therefore their tastes help to create atmosphere or reveal weaknesses of some kind. Apart from the overblown opulence of the Sternwoods, with the cloying smell of orchids – 'Their flesh is too like the flesh of men. And their perfume has the rotten sweetness of a prostitute' – and the deathly white hangings, there is the magnificence of real riches which allows the wealthy to hide their double-dealing, cover up their corruption, give an outward show of pomp and power to hush up crimes from the press and police. Only the private investigator, spurred on more by his own almost chivalric sense of ethics rather than by the paltry pay from whoever retains him, is likely to see the truth behind the mask of money.

In *The Long Goodbye* it is the fabulously wealthy and powerful newspaper proprietor Harlan Potter who tries to cover up the murder of his daughter because he is a man who shuns publicity. It goes deeper than that: Potter is a rich man – 'a hundred millions' – who uses his wealth to live as a recluse in the Howard Hughes manner. He loathes the American social system, planned obsolescence, the quest for material possessions; Chandler allows him several paragraphs to express his philosophy. Paradoxically, Potter is surrounded by the symbols of financial success for which the bourgeoisie strive. His threatening interview with Marlowe takes place in the intimidating atmosphere of an imitation French chateau, a gross, gloomy piece of architectural phantasmagoria which Potter bought for his eldest daughter:

> It was the damndest-looking house I ever saw. It was a square, grey box three stories high, with a mansard roof, steeply sloped and broken by twenty or thirty double dormer windows with a lot of wedding-cake decorations around them and between them. The entrance had double stone pillars on each side but the cream of the joint was an outside spiral staircase with a stone railing, topped by a tower room from which there must have been a view the whole length of the lake.

Chandler had much to draw from when it came to describing the architectural follies of Los Angeles: Greco-Roman, Byzantine, Moorish, Gothic, Baroque, French, Dutch, Spanish, English colonial. Most of them are built for outward show, to lend dignity and solidity to lives which are often empty and lubricious.

The stars of Hollywood, including the great producers, directors and executives, were the main occupants of these mansions, although oddly enough Chandler makes less use of the film colony as a source of skulduggery than one might expect.

In *The Little Sister* an up-and-coming film star is being blackmailed; the apartment where she lives is, for Hollywood, comparatively modest:

> The apartment house was over on Doheny Boulevard, just down from the Strip. It was really two buildings, one behind the other, loosely connected by a floored patio with a fountain and a room built over the arch.

The fountain is the only concession, there, to luxury, although when Marlowe crosses the patio he sees 'a big ornamental pool full of goldfish', as well as 'a couple of stone seats and a lawn swing'.

Very restrained for Hollywood, and naturally, the lack of vulgar show is, for the reader, a careful indication of the star's status. Today there are a few duplex apartments 'down the hill from the Strip' and the homes on that section of Doheny are fairly new apartment blocks. Chandler's Mavis Weld, the aspiring star, could still live there, and Chandler's specific use of location would still be as telling about her status as it was in 1949, the year in which *The Little Sister* was first published.

Much more opulent, but every bit as reflective of personality and social position, are the offices of Mavis's agent, Sheridan Ballou. After passing through a ritzy reception room and further anterooms, through 'double doors of heavy black glass with silver peacocks etched into the panes', Marlowe is ushered into an office

> that had everything in it but a swimming pool. It was two stories high, surrounded by a balcony loaded with bookshelves. There was a concert grand Steinway in the corner and a lot of glass and bleached wood furniture and a desk about the size of a badminton court and chairs and couches and tables....

Give or take the black glass doors, there are contemporary Hollywood agents' offices that reflect equal munificence and, by implication, the importance of the agent himself and the clients he handles.

The 9000 Building is a skyscraper which dominates Sunset Strip at its busiest point. The glass and steel monolith houses suites of agents' offices which are not far removed from the self-conscious show of Sheridan Ballou. If Chandler were writing today he would probably invent his own 9000 Building with an interior decorated with European plunderings – Renaissance cherubs on the elevator ceilings, gilded candelabra dispensing the services of the General Electric Company in a lobby muted by panels of stained glass. Perhaps he would locate it a couple of blocks away from the prototype, just as Marlowe's office in the fictional Cahuenga Building in *Farewell, My Lovely* is a facsimile of office buildings on the corner of Hollywood Boulevard and Ivar which are, in fact, still there in their solid thirties stone cladding. Marlowe's own office was dingy and dusty, situated in a building much lower down the social scale. But architecturally it had been fashioned for the rich, and still stands in all its Art-Deco splendour.

Bullock's department store, unchanged since the day when Chandler first mentioned it in *The Big Sleep*, has a commanding position on that

Bullock's department store on Wilshire Boulevard, one of the Art-Deco glories of Los Angeles

Chandler fans argue about which office blocks in Hollywood were the ones Marlowe used. This one is at the junction of Hollywood and Highland Avenue

Left: *In* Farewell My Lovely *Marlowe says his office is 'on Hollywood Boulevard, near Ivar'. This thirties building, still there, is probably the one Chandler had in mind*

part of Wilshire Boulevard known as the Miracle Mile, the bronze-green multi-towered configuration decorated with the stylized figures and geometrical shapes typical of the period. In the thirties Bullock's was the last word in modern department-store design; even now its interior has fortunately escaped alteration. 'The violet light at the top of Bullock's green-tinged tower' is still visible from 'the east entrance to the parking lot' where Marlowe so specifically paid off the pathetic Agnes Lozelle with 'two C notes' in *The Big Sleep*. Only the cars look different today, and sometimes even they can be in period.

Farther west on Sunset Boulevard stands another beautiful Art-Deco apartment building where, in all probability, several of Bullock's rich customers lived and which would have made a fine setting for any of Chandler's double-dealing socialite ladies. The building is called Sunset Tower, located on that part of the Strip which, some years ago, was the favourite parade ground of the hippy hordes who turned the twenty-four-hour scene into a mardi gras, outraging Hollywood's older citizens. Chandler uses the building in *The Big Sleep* as a point of reference for an abandoned car found nearby; he also gives it a fictitious twin – Bryson Tower – on Wilshire Boulevard, a little farther south. He is, however, at pains to give it oriental overtones, possibly so that his rather disapproving description of its luxury might not offend the residents.

Sunset Tower itself – whatever it may have been in Chandler's day – is now a beautiful period showpiece, one of the best in Los Angeles. Fourteen floors high, it is painted pale ochre and decorated at the top with bas-reliefs of modernistic figures and motifs. The overall shape is reminiscent of those radiogram consoles of the thirties. It is to Los Angeles what the Chrysler Building is to New York and one must hope that, in a town of transient and ephemeral features, there is some form of preservation order in existence that will protect it. No matter what it might have symbolized for Philip Marlowe – ill-gotten gains, suspect wealth, an overdecorated setting for the oversexed and underestimated cuties with whom he was so often embroiled – he would have been the first to condemn the big business operators who might want to replace it with something else.

Down in the City of Los Angeles itself, an area as distinct within Greater Los Angeles as the City of London is within Greater London, is the beautiful mid-thirties Union Station, still resplendent with Spanish-style tiles and archways. Except for the different size and

The beautiful Art-Deco Sunset Tower mentioned in The Big Sleep. *It has recently been restored to pristine period perfection*

The Union Pacific railroad station in downtown Los Angeles no longer handles the traffic it once did, but it still looks exactly the same as when Chandler described it in the novel Playback. Compare the contemporary photograph (above) with the one taken in 1939

disposition of the palms and jacaranda trees around it, it looks exactly the same as when Marlowe sat in the big waiting room tailing the girl he had been commissioned to follow in *Playback*.

She had just stepped off the Santa Fe Railroad Super Chief, the great, glittering, streamlined, transcontinental train that used to link LA with central USA, bringing the stars and celebrities to Chandlertown before the airlines took the trade. There are now only a few trains a day, one or two going north and east, one or two, like the one which Marlowe caught, bound for San Diego in the south. The huge waiting rooms are nearly empty, the coffee shop and the bar and the bookstall have few customers....

4
EVERYTHING ELSE WAS JUNK

If America embodies the extremes of wealth and poverty within its society, then Los Angeles contains the ultimate of these extremes. From the extravagant splendours of the film-star homes and the pompous piles of industrial moguls to the impoverished ethnic communities, the derelicts of the downtown Skid Row and the human detritus of the waterfront, every form of rags to riches and back again is on display. New York and a dozen other US cities, of course, have similar examples of social and material inequality, but they are neither so contiguous nor so cruelly illuminated as they are under the Californian sun.

Marlowe was in fairly constant contact with the super-rich, either as his clients or as shadowy, elusive figures trying to obstruct his work, but he rarely had much to do with the really impoverished, the down and outs. Marlowe's disadvantaged are mostly the old – decrepit desk clerks in dim hotels, alcoholics trying to forget their descent down the social scale, the outcasts forced to bum a living on the fringes of crime – people who, in today's socially self-conscious terminology, might elevate themselves with the word 'hustler'. Chandler never used the word. In contemporary America, 'hustling' has a spurious glamour, part of the same romanticized aura that surrounds airline pilots, professional gamblers, rodeo riders – even private detectives. It carries overtones of action and danger, of modern buccaneering. Marlowe would never be taken in by such self-delusion; he knew that the poor, though often in need of protection, could be as venal, as vicious, as the rich; it was just a matter of degree. 'Two C notes' was enough for Agnes Lozelle to give vital information in *The Big Sleep*: five bucks was the price demanded by Peoria Smith in *The Little Sister* for Mavis Weld's unlisted telephone number; a bottle of booze was enough to loosen the tongue of Jessie Florian in *Farewell, My Lovely*. 'Money sharpens the memory,' Marlowe said to her. 'So does liquor,' Jessie replied, accepting Marlowe's bourbon.

Chandler had an ironic eye for lavish display and he also meticulously recorded the squalor of louche Los Angeles.

No. 499 had a shallow, painted front porch on which fire wood and cane rockers loafed dissolutely, held together with wire and the moisture of the beach air. The green shades over the lower windows of the house were two-thirds down and full of cracks. Beside the front door there was a large printed sign 'No Vacancies'. That had been there a long time too. It had got jaded and fly-specked.

That is the entrance to a sleazy apartment house in *The Little Sister*. Inside Marlowe notices other indications of general delapidation and decay – a dirty garbage pail, a box full of empty liquor bottles, an overstuffed chair scarred by cigarette burns, a greasy cushion cover. Private filth is similarly documented:

1644 West 54th Place was a dried-out brown house with a dried-out brown lawn in front of it. On the porch stood one lonely wooden rocker and the afternoon breeze made the unpruned shoots of last year's poinsettias tap-tap against the cracked stucco walk.

Small, wood-frame bungalows are a very typical feature of all Los Angeles residential districts, especially the poorer ones. Chandler often made use of them as the homes of secondary characters such as the maid, Agatha, in the short story 'The King in Yellow' and as Jessie Florian's house in Farewell My Lovely

That is the approach to alcoholic Jessie Florian's house in *Farewell, My Lovely*. Inside, again, the theme of grime and neglect is continued:

> Everything else was junk – dirty overstuffed pieces, a wooden rocker that matched the one on the porch, a square arch into a dining room with a stained table, finger marks all over the door to the kitchen beyond. A couple of frayed lamps with once gaudy shades that were now as gay as superannuated streetwalkers.

Later, the general accumulation of frowsiness makes the hard-boiled cop accompanying Marlowe exclaim: 'What a way to live!'

Very often it is Marlowe's olfactory nerve which registers the rottenness, rather than his retina. Foul air, stale odours, decomposing flesh, sweat, cigarette smoke, liquor fumes, cooking smells, all accentuated by the persistent heat, are frequent indications of human impurity, the stench of putrescence signifying inward decadence. Marlowe himself is fairly fastidious: the dust on his office desk is indicative only of his modest means, not personal slovenliness or lax morals. It is one thing not to be able to afford a daily office cleaner; it is another to wear a shirt with a grimy collar.

In Los Angeles today Marlowe would be able to find even more examples of a soiled city than he did twenty years ago, from the generally unkempt youth (one speculates on Marlowe's likely comments on the lank hair and dirty bare feet so common today on Sunset Strip and Hollywood Boulevard!) to the eye-searing, lung-spotting smog that clings to the Los Angeles basin. He was beginning to get an inkling of it – the smog, anyway – back in the fifties, when the first freeways were being built and the post-war boom was filling the highways with bug-eyed, fintailed monsters of cars.

The rapid growth of Los Angeles, the encroachment of prospective building and speculative real estate to house the constant migration to Southern California, meant not only that large parts of long-established areas were abandoned to decay, but that much of what was thrown up so hastily became instant slums. In the 1950s, a terrifying sign displaying continuously changing, electrically illuminated numerals told of the minute-by-minute population increase as yet another person crossed the state border to take up residence. Hollywood itself, partly responsible, plummeted from being the glamour city of the twenties and became dowdy through overpopulation, a centre swamped by the hopeful but impecunious. As the rich moved out to less-developed areas, the poor – as is the way – took over, the poorest of all being the Negroes. Later they were joined by illegal immigrants from Mexico, but the twin problems – racial equality for the downtrodden Blacks, a flood of Latin Americans looking for work – had not reached, in Marlowe's time, the major proportions of today. Even so, the coloured population had begun to move to the districts previously favoured by 'white trash'.

'It was one of the mixed blocks over on Central Avenue, the blocks that are not yet all negro.' Thus runs the opening line of *Farewell, My Lovely*, and immediately Chandler has set his scene, an area where the poor Blacks and whites overlap, where cheap crooks and petty crime are commonplace, where the huge Moose Malloy goes looking for his lost torch singer Velma, only to find that the Blacks have taken over Florian's dine-and-dice emporium during his eight years in prison.

In 1940, when the novel was written, Chandler was more or less in accord with his reactionary readers. Negroes (Marlowe has no compunction about using the colloquialism 'niggers') represented not only the deterioration associated with poverty but demoralization, degeneracy, depravity too. Moose's first action is to throw out of Florian's a Negro to whom he contemptuously refers as 'a dinge'. Chandler writes of the 'thin narrow-shouldered brown youth' as 'it'. Moose then goes on to flatten the barman with his fist and shoot the manager. What matter? They were only 'dinge'.

Nowadays, in Los Angeles, Negroes can enter almost any smart, upper-class establishment – the city has even had a Negro mayor – and they are not necessarily the most deprived of the ethnic groups. Today's Blacks have the (doubtful) advantages of civil rights, and the real social losers are the poor Mexicans, generally disdained, in turn, by the Negroes.

The Mexicans – and other South Americans – are exploitable in Los Angeles because many of them live there illegally. Hundreds of thousands cross the border – just a couple of hours' drive away, a few miles south of San Diego – and make for the city. There, they can lose themselves in the various and vast no-man's-land residential areas, squat in shanty towns, move from one squalid shack to another, even live alfresco in that benevolent climate. A few have relations or contacts who provide some form of subsistence; those who do not are immediately exploitable as cheap labour – there are many factories where the workers are all Spanish speaking – in divers forms of light industry, in cheap restaurants and snack bars and as domestics.

It is a commonplace to have domestic help delivered to the door in a mini-bus. The tightly packed vehicles circulate the well-to-do areas at about 8 a.m., dropping off Mexican women at elegant front doors. Often only the driver speaks English, interpreting the household duties and chores before driving off again. In the evening he is back, to collect the Mexicans and the money and take a substantial cut. All these people receive far less than the going rate for workers protected by unions.

The area around Washington Boulevard and Central Avenue still contains some fine period pieces like these 'American Gothic' houses. Many of them are now rooming houses in what has become a predominantly Mexican district. When Chandler wrote the opening lines of the short story 'Pick up on Noon Street' and the novel Farewell My Lovely *the blacks were taking over from the poor whites. Central Avenue runs several miles south to the huge black district of Watts*

Being illegal means having no redress. Even so, their standard of living in Los Angeles is positively luxurious compared with the conditions they have left behind.

Of course, for many who cross the border (some crammed in the boots of cars that regularly crash through the Border Patrol checkpoints at risk to life and limb) it is petty – and not so petty – crime that is the means by which they can achieve the material success they pursue so desperately. For the Mexican, this usually means drugs. Marijuana is the main substance, but heroin and cocaine arrive in increasing quantities, the USA–Mexico border being the last obstacle on a journey that may have begun in Turkey or Southeast Asia. The narcotics come in knapsacks on the backs of trekkers taking the innumerable mountain trails; in motorcycles and cars and trucks and campers, sometimes stashed under the seat, sometimes concealed in elaborate secret compartments; in outboard dinghies, fast motorboats, offshore cruisers, fishing boats, elegant yachts; in light aircraft, charter aircraft, the luggage aboard regular airliners – even in radio-controlled model aircraft. Some of the stratagems which have been developed make James Bond look like an amateur; but whatever the means employed, it is invariably the poor Mexicans who do the dirtiest and most dangerous work.

The same problems existed in Chandler's day, although not on the same scale, and he made occasional use of the Mexicans and references to the drug scene in several of Marlowe's cases. Even then the Mexicans were usually cast in the role of the dangerous knife-wielding servant – houseboy, chauffeur or bodyguard – never as the smooth top operator: that was reserved for the upper-echelon white trash. In *The Long Goodbye* there is a sleek Latin houseboy named Candy. He is obsessively protective of his murderess mistress, patrols the house as silently as a cat, keeps a flick knife handy in his immaculate white monkey jacket. He is there more as a prop, a piece of fancy scene-setting, a bit of colour, than as a character of any real significance. Chandler knew his kind would be familiar in many Los Angeles upper-class homes, less obtrusive than a Negro servant and, for the reader then, rather more sinister. Other Mexicans make brief appearances in the Chandler stories, usually as servants – waiters, doormen, hotel clerks:

> The door of the porter's room beside the elevators opened and the little Mexican night operator came out in street clothes. He looked at Tony with a quiet sideways look out of eyes the colour of dried-out chestnuts. ('I'll Be Waiting')

Whatever significance that 'quiet sideways look' with its inference of sly observation, Marlowe's Mexicans usually know their place, like the modern immigrant who knows how lucky he is to have grafted himself onto the rich Californian way of life and rarely jeopardizes his job or spurious residential status by stepping out of line.

Not so the Negroes, who can get uppity, even in the more repressive Chandlertown of the forties. I have remarked on Moose Malloy's prompt dispatch of two or three who crossed his path, and Marlowe himself is permitted an ironic comment on one who got his come-uppance. "'Well, all he did was kill a negro," I said, "I guess that's only a misdemeanour.'" Despite the passage of time – and the passage of various civil rights bills through Congress – there are still hundreds of people in Los Angeles who would echo Marlowe's ironic quip. The liberalism of the radical chic is literally only skin deep and at WASP dinner tables and cocktail parties the mask is often dropped.

The memory of the Watts riots has not faded either, any more than the running sore of Watts itself, a blemish on the face of Los Angeles. It lies to the southwest of the city, stretching for mile after mile, becoming progressively more depressing. It does not have the teeming squalor of Harlem, but it is dusty and dreary, seeming more so in the searching sunlight. There is a pathetic attempt to ape the affluence of white Los Angeles, seen in the seedy respectability and the weary attempts at keeping up appearances in the face of deprivation and destitution. Chandler would have some accurate phrases for it, for if Marlowe were operating now he would surely have had some call to visit the locality or at least make reference to it, so frequently does it figure in the modern Los Angeles scene. Neither is it unlikely that a latter-day Marlowe would have had a Mexican or a Negro client: they have too large and important a part in the life of the contemporary city for one of them at least not to drift into Marlowe's (probably still dusty) office on Hollywood and Ivar and ask him to trace a missing boyfriend or piece of jewellery.

5

A FAINT SMELL OF OCEAN

Santa Monica, one of the oldest settlements of Los Angeles, is in the centre of the Bay area which is the model for Chandler's Bay City. It has five or six miles of waterfront with wide yellow sands which accommodate tens of thousands of Angelinos at weekends. It has a rickety pier, the only one of several to survive since the twenties, built on wooden piles which still support a very old carousel brought from Vienna,* several cheap fish restaurants, one or two seaside souvenir shops and a half-hearted fun fair. It is a poor substitute for the big dipper that three or four decades ago raised its lunatically looped outline over the Pacific. Chandler's Bay City is raffish and corrupt, and despite a change of profile, the same sense of danger and delapidation lingers.

In 1975 Santa Monica celebrated the one hundredth anniversary of its official incorporation as a city. Americans tend to bestow the word 'city' on almost any small collection of homes, bank, drug store and gas station; even single shops tend to call themselves 'cities' – Music City, Flower City, Junk City, Book City – though perhaps a Chamber of Commerce sets the final seal of recognition. But the history of Santa Monica is one of the oldest of the Los Angeles area.

One of the main causes of crime in Chandlertown is corruption; the murders which Marlowe investigates are usually just steps along the way, incidental to the uncovering of political or commercial graft, and it is Chandler's Bay City that is frequently the centre of corruption – far more than Hollywood or Beverly Hills or the city of Los Angeles itself. And at the centre of the centre it is not only the big businessmen or even the gangsters who inhabit the area – both in reality and in Chandler's fiction – but the police.

Marlowe's attitude to policemen is equivocal – he was, we know, an ex-cop himself: he recognizes that they are frequently set up to be shot down, that they are necessarily tough, that they arc overworked and underpaid and consequently open to being bought, that they can be

*Seen by the cinema-going public in *The Sting*.

manipulated by politicians and big-business bosses who are even more open to corruption than the police themselves – and also that they are likely to obstruct Marlowe himself in serving his clients. There is usually a wary tolerance between Marlowe and the average cop, and he finds it helps to have one or two well disposed towards him. He frequently needs to sail close to the wind of legality (i.e. delaying, if not actually failing to report, a murder), but he will not, at least at the start of a case, put at risk his licence to operate as a private investigator by deliberately flouting the law.

There is a distinct contrast between Marlowe's recognition of the tired, harassed, undervalued City of Los Angeles policeman and his smart, smug, almost openly corrupt opposite number in Bay City.

In *The Little Sister*, Detective Lieutenant Christy French personifies the Los Angeles City Police. He is tough, tired, not above intimidating a suspect with physical violence, views the world with sour cynicism and looks upon Marlowe as a two-timer capable of murder when pushed to it. Chandler allows him a speech which encapsulates pretty well the sophisticated acceptance that the average cop comes close to being a crook in uniform:

'We're coppers and everybody hates our guts. And as if we didn't have enough trouble, we have to have you [Marlowe]. As if we didn't get pushed around enough by the guys in the corner offices, the City Hall Gang, the day Chief, the night Chief, the Chamber of Commerce, His Honour the Mayor in his panelled office four times as big as the three lousy rooms the whole homicide staff has to work out of. As if we didn't have to handle one hundred and fourteen homicides last year out of three rooms that don't have enough chairs for the whole duty squad to sit down at once. We spend our lives turning over dirty underwear and sniffing rotten teeth. We go up dark stairways to get a gun punk with a skinful of hop and sometimes we don't get all the way up, and our wives wait dinner that night and all the other nights. We don't come home any more. And nights we do come home so goddam tired we can't eat or sleep or even read the lies the papers print about us, so we lie awake in the dark in a cheap house on a cheap street and listen to the drunks down the block having fun. And just about the time we drop off the phone rings and we get up and start all over again. Nothing we do is right, not ever. Not once. If we get a confession, we beat it out of the guy, they say, and some shyster calls us Gestapo in court and sneers at us when we muddle our grammar. If we make a mistake they put us back in uniform on Skid Row and we spend the nice cool summer evenings picking drunks out of the gutter and being yelled at by whores and taking knives away from grease-balls in zoot suits.'

That diatribe reads almost as if Chandler had taken it down verbatim from some jaundiced, disillusioned cop, too far into his career to get out, who wanted to make sure the public realized that a policeman's lot is not a happy one. Alternatively, Chandler may have written it because it counterbalanced the brutal, repellent Captain Gregorius in *The Long Goodbye*:

> a type of copper that is getting rarer but by no means extinct, the kind that solves crimes with the bright light, the soft sap,* the kick to the kidneys, the knee to the groin, the night stick to the base of the spine.

He has handcuffs tightened on Marlowe's wrists until they go numb; he throws hot coffee at Marlowe, he hits him on the side of the cheek 'with a fist like a piece of iron' and finally spits in his face. Nasty, but not, perhaps, so odious as the fat chief of Bay City Police, John Wax (like so many in the novels, an evocative name), in *Farewell, My Lovely*. Wax's henchmen have already beaten up Marlowe, but the chief is too clever to use physical violence himself. He is doing nicely, anyway, obviously taking bribes that make him an altogether sleeker proposition than the hard-boiled toughs downtown.

> He was a hammered down heavyweight with short pink hair and a pink scalp glistening through it. He had small, hungry, heavy-lidded eyes, as restless as fleas. He wore a suit of fawn-coloured flannel, a coffee-coloured shirt and tie, a diamond ring, a diamond-studded lodge pin in his lapel.... He turned in his chair and crossed his thick legs ... that let me see handspun lisle socks and English brogues that looked as if they had been pickled in port wine. Counting what I couldn't see and not counting his wallet he had half a grand on him. I figured his wife had money.

That is a typical Marlowe wisecrack, a deliberately *faux-naïf* remark; Marlowe knew too many corrupt cops to believe it really was like that. If Chandler based Chief Wax on some particular real-life case in which a police chief was getting a rake-off from various rackets, it probably took place in another area of Los Angeles. Be that as it may, Chandler anticipated a scandal that came to light only three years after he died, when it was alleged that widespread gambling and prostitution was being conducted in Santa Monica while the police conveniently looked away. The police chief was sacked, reinstated, then, citing 'health reasons', retired soon afterwards. Two *private investigators* were hired to report on the charges that had been made and found them to be substantially true. The story would have made Chandler smile – he may have known about it long before it broke in the press.

For all the conjecture about how Chandler would have mined latter-day material, he certainly made astute and effective use of what there was to hand.

*A form of blackjack that leaves no mark.

The offshore gambling ships, run by the racketeer Brunette, which provide the climactic scenes of *Farewell, My Lovely*, read like fiction; in fact they were a real feature of the Bay area from the thirties to the fifties. Chandler has little need to disguise them, apart from changing their names.

> The *Royal Crown* seemed to ride as steady as a pier on its four hausers. Its landing stage was lit up like a theatre marquee. Then all this faded into remoteness and another, older, smaller boat began to sneak out of the night towards us. It was not much to look at. A converted sea-going freighter with scummed and rusted plates, the superstructure cut down to the boatdeck level, and above that two stumpy masts just high enough for a radio antenna. There was light on the *Montecito* also, and music floated across the wet dark sea.

Those are pretty accurate descriptions of the gambling ships anchored beyond the three-mile limit in the summer of 1938. (*Farewell, My Lovely* was first published in 1940.) They were owned by a racketeer called Cornero, a man who had previously prospered by rum-running up the coast from Mexico during the Prohibition years. When a judge's ruling finally closed Cornero's floating casinos, he went off to run a famous hotel in Las Vegas. Chandler's gambling boss Brunette coincidentally ran a gambling hall in Nevada's other fun town, Reno.

Most of Chandler's portrayal of Bay City is still recognizable. His scruffy promenade area around the pier is pieced together in short paragraphs and phrases like a mosaic:

> Outside the narrow street fumed, the sidewalks swarmed with fat stomachs. Across the street a bingo parlour was going full blast and beside it a couple of sailors with girls were coming out of a photographer's shop. . . . The voice of the hot dog merchant split the dusk like an axe . . . there was a faint smell of ocean. Not very much, but as if they had kept this much just to remind people this had once been a clean open beach where the waves came in and creamed and the wind blew and you could smell something besides the hot fat and cold sweat . . . beyond the smell of hot fat and popcorn and the shrill children and the barkers in the peepshows. . . .

The smell of hot fat still lingers around the hot dog stands and the popcorn counters, the fat stomachs and shrill children still throng the sidewalk; the bingo parlours and peepshows tend to have given way to garish beach boutiques and shops selling remnants of psychedelia. The feeling of human despoliation persists.

During the late sixties the hippies descended to play their guitars, smoke pot, drop acid, freak out and make out on the beach and in the ramshackle apartments also lived in by equally impoverished senior citizens. Only a few hippies remain today, and fewer senior citizens;

they are content to play chess in the sun and watch the self-conscious athletes performing on the parallel bars, swings and rings of adjacent Muscle Beach. Part of the waterfront has been given a new elegance; a big 1930s apartment block, almost on the sands, which must have been familiar to Chandler, has been repainted and restored to its currently fashionable period smartness.

A little farther inland is another well-preserved building which must have been one of the local architectural showpieces in Chandler's day, the City Hall and Police Department of Santa Monica, built in 1939. Doubtless not to make Bay City Hall – and its public servants – too identifiable, Chandler persists in describing the previous building, built in 1902 for the 'bargain' price of $40,000:

> It was a cheap-looking building for so prosperous a town. It looked more like something out of the Bible Belt. Bums sat unmolested in a long row on the retaining wall that kept the front lawn – now mostly Bermuda grass – from falling into the street. The building was of three stories and had an old belfry at the top and the bell still hanging in the belfry.

Only the addition of minor detail could make the description more exact.

The 'modern' Santa Monica City Hall has itself become a period piece, a long, low, white building which is a perfect example of thirties municipal architecture, embellished round the main portico with colourful tiles that add a Spanish–Mexican flavour. Inside there is more tiling and some splendid murals depicting the main events in the locality's history, from the first landing by Cabrillo to the famous four-month-long round-the-world flight undertaken by four Douglas aircraft from the aerospace factory established at Santa Monica's Clover Field. The new Police Department was added to the rear of the building some years later, so perhaps Chandler was right in placing his smooth and unctuous John Wax in the old 'Bible Belt' building. Chandler invariably worked close to the bone of reality.

If, in more recent years, there have not been big scandals involving

---

Above left: *Santa Monica (Chandler's Bay City) and the sleazy promenade area near Santa Monica pier is graphically described in* Farewell My Lovely. *In the sixties the area was invaded by hippies and it still retains its raffish ambience. Recently the big thirties block facing the beach has been renovated, and it now looks just as it did in Chandler's day*

Left: *The attractive Santa Monica City Hall built in the late thirties*

police corruption in Bay City or elsewhere in Los Angeles, it may still be taken as a persistent concomitant of all police forces all over the world – in varying degrees, of course. In Chandler's era corruption and graft had been brought to the fore – all over America – by Prohibition. It gave a sudden, tremendous impetus not only to the idea, and practice, of policemen being bought as a result of the widespread avoidance of such a basically ridiculous diktat but also to the gangsterism attendant upon it. Chicago, of course, suffered from, and epitomized, gangsterism most, but the Mafia-led malfeasance and mayhem affected every part of the continent. Chandler made use of gangsterism in some of his pre-Marlowe short stories, but it was the legacy bequeathed to American society, the acceptance of widespread corruption extending from City Hall to the cop on the beat, that was such grist to Marlowe's mill.

What Chandler's cops and his private investigator(s) did *not* have to contend with was the wave of nationwide hostility to the police that became such an element in the social revolutions in the sixties. Being 'busted' and beaten by the 'pigs' became almost a fashionable commonplace, especially among the young, who were part of a rising crime rate that would have amazed Chandler and Marlowe.

The hippy phenomenon which mushroomed in the sixties (an offspring of the beatniks of the late fifties, a sociological feature which Chandler would no doubt have made use of had he lived) made Southern California its Mecca. It was another trek to the West, using mini-buses instead of covered wagons, with the proximity of Mexico and its easy supply of marijuana part of the attraction. When San Francisco's Haight Ashbury area became too hot, the hordes settled around Venice and Santa Monica; Bay City became Hash and Hassle City and Chief John Wax and his boys would have had, paradoxically, rich pickings from the more sinister forces which manipulated the vulnerable flower children.

Marlowe would have been in something of a quandary: nothing that one gleans from reading about Chandler's almost romantic incorruptible quiet squares with the amorality of the dropouts. The generation gap between Marlowe and the hippies would have been at least as wide as the morality gap between Marlowe and Chief Wax; in that respect Chandlertown today presents unfamiliar territory to a poor shamus who thought he had sorted out just where he stood twenty years ago.

As a matter of literary interest, Bay City has been the home and inspiration of other distinguished writers. Christopher Isherwood has lived in Santa Monica canyon for thirty-six years. His description of the area in *Exhumations* (1966), in a passage called 'The Shore', would have pleased Chandler. Isherwood called it 'an area of romantic delapidation ... not so much a waterfront as a background washed by waves'.

Another writer, whose sojourn in Santa Monica produced several stories located in Los Angeles, is Gavin Lambert. In particular *The Slide Area*, the title referring to the crumbling cliffs along the Santa Monica coastline, is a series of short stories which carry graphic descriptions of that part of the city.

But sometimes a landmark disappears, like the old pier between Santa Monica and Venice. Replacing the shabby arcades of obsolete peep-shows and makeshift booths is a bright new pleasure cape, clean and synthetic.

That, too, has now gone.

6
ONE-MAN DEATH WATCH

Violence is an accepted part of the American way of life and an essential part of the detective story. It is not a gratuitous element, as it might be in other societies and genres, and Chandlertown is a perfect embodiment of both. The town and the violence there have grown almost beyond recognition in the past thirty years.

Chandler's early short stories – in which the prototypes of Marlowe appear – contain, surprisingly, as much if not more violence than the novels. He was aware of this, did not, in fact, think that violence should necessarily play a big part in the story, and wanted to write a novel in which *no* murder took place. He was aware that the *threat* of violence, the gun glinting under electric light, the menacing presence of a gangster's bodyguard, a hint of intimidation in police interrogation procedures, was as effective as the act of violence itself. Nevertheless such acts were and are there, both before and after Marlowe was conceived, and they reflect the lawlessness that has always been a part of Chandlertown.

Shoot-outs between a private investigator and gangsters are frequent occurrences in the short stories:

> Erno's lips twitched under his shiny little moustache. Two guns went off at the same time. Landrey swayed like a tree hit by a gust of wind; the heavy roar of his .45 sounded again, muffled a little by cloth and the nearness of his body. ('Blackmailers Don't Shoot')

There follows a description of both men's dying falls. Later:

> He steadied himself; the Luger talked twice, very rapidly. The blond boy's arm jerked up ... his eyes widened, his mouth came open in a yell of pain. Then he whirled, wrenched the door open and pitched straight out on the landing with a crash.... Something loomed in the doorway, Mallory heaved sideways, firing blindly at the door. But the sound of the Luger was overborne by the terrific flat booming of a shotgun. Searing flame stabbed down Mallory's right side. Mardonne got the rest of the load.... A sawed-off shotgun dumped itself in through the open door. A thick-bellied man in shirtsleeves eased himself down

in the doorframe, clutching and rolling as he fell. A strangled sob came out of his mouth, and blood spread on the pleated front of a dress shirt. ('Blackmailers Don't Shoot')

Two shoot-outs (there are other shootings) in one short story – more violence than in any of the novels. It is probable that readers of pulp magazines wanted that sort of thing as well; later Chandler's growing expertise as a writer enabled him to sustain tension and interest without resort to scenes of bloody action. Also the short stories are closer in time to the gangster days of Prohibition when armed confrontation between rival thugs was more commonplace than in the novels, whose length permits the comparatively slow unravelling of crimes committed for different motivational reasons. Either way, Chandlertown had it all.

One of the short stories also carries a rare instance of pure sadism, a huge gorilla-like Negro who enjoys strangling people:

He hit Pete Anglich again with the gun, then suddenly he jammed it into a side pocket and his two big hands shot out, clamped themselves on Pete Anglich's throat. 'When they's tough I likes to squeeze 'em,' he said, almost softly. ('Pick-Up on Noon Street')

That type of character has now become almost *de rigueur* in crime fiction.

Chandler could certainly find instances of crime which he could use fictionally simply by picking up a copy of the *Los Angeles Times*. He employed the well-worn literary precedent of absorbing life into the novelist's art; Stendhal used an actual murder case as the basis of his plot in *Scarlet and Black*. Theodore Dreiser did the same in *An American Tragedy*. Chandler found the skeletons for his crimes in its underworld activities when they surfaced in newsprint. Nowadays a crime writer can sit behind a desk and watch newsmen photographing shoot-outs and interviewing the killers and survivors on television; he can see the gory details of mass murders in his sitting room. Creatively inspiring? The private agony of the individual has become entertainment – vicarious and cathartic – for the masses. From the fiction fringes of Truman Capote's *In Cold Blood* to the exploitation of the cruelty, horror and tragedies of the concentration camps for second-hand sadism in pornographic magazines, man's inhumanity to man has often been the substance of literature and theatre. Television has the unique advantage of showing both sides of the crime coin; heads and you see the real thing muted only by the selective eye of the cameraman; tails and you have Harry O or Rockford or Cannon, private eyes who are, in one way or another, direct descendants of Marlowe.

Most of the murders that Marlowe encountered happened at night.

Today – evidenced in print and on film – violence occurs as frequently in the daylight. Although Chandler knew that murder was just as likely to happen at noon as at midnight, most of Marlowe's encounters with murderers and their victims take place after dark.

In the *old* Chandlertown the atmospherics of darkness, the killer in the shadows – or at least behind the curtain – often added immeasurably to the sense of menace. That famous Chandler phrase, 'the smell of fear', which serves as the title to the collected short stories as well as for a recent London season of *cinema noir* (only a few of which were Chandler screenplays or direct versions of the novels), is so much more effective under low-key studio lighting or in the descriptive passages of the books.

> I went up the steps slowly. It was a soft night with a little haze in the air. The trees on the hill hardly moved. No breeze. I unlocked the door and pushed it part way open and then stopped. The door was about ten inches open from the frame. It was dark inside, there was no sound. But I had the feeling that the room beyond was not empty. Perhaps a spring squeaked faintly or I caught the gleam of a white jacket across the room. Perhaps on a warm still night like this one the room beyond the door was not warm enough, but still enough. Perhaps there was a drifting smell of man on the air. (*Farewell, My Lovely*)

The smell of fear: it is a perfectly calculated passage, using the location evocatively – the 'warm still night', the sinister suggestion of an unnatural chill in the unlit room beyond the partly open door, the sense of death waiting in the dark. Again:

> A darkened window slid down inch by inch, only some shifting of light on the glass showing it moved.... Then silence for a little while, except for the rain and the quiet throbbing motor of the car. Then the house door crawled open, a deeper blackness in the black night. A figure showed in it cautiously, something white around the neck. It was her collar. She came out on the porch stiffly, a wooden woman. I caught the pale shine of her silver wig. Canino came crouched methodically behind her. It was so deadly it was almost funny. (*The Big Sleep*)

Not funny, actually, but frightening – and a gift to any director. It is much easier to startle, thrill and control an audience so that there is a sudden surge of blood to make the heart race and the hairs of the head and forearms bristle with horror when night shadows hide the waiting danger.

In contemporary Chandlertown there is a blatant disregard for such contrived refinements. There is blood on the sunlit sidewalks, stake-outs on Main Street at noon, quiet killers in busy shopping precincts and crowded parking lots. Recent, more sensational crimes – the motiveless blood lust, say, of the Charles Manson gang – would make poor copy for the elaborate structure of crime detection fiction, whatever poetic licence might be employed. Chandler's hoods always had a reason, even if it *was* just the repetitious one of material gain; wealth and power – which are so often synonymous – have, after all, been the main motives for murder from *Hamlet* to *The High Window*. Only love – and its various perverted forms – has given an equally consistent impetus to homicide. But love is a theme Raymond Chandler uses only sparingly.

Los Angeles in the thirties and forties was the scene of several sensational crimes, and one of the most widely reported was the murder of film star Thelma Todd. The crime was unsolved and had in it numerous elements which are found in Chandler's stories of detection.

Miss Todd lived with a film director in an apartment over a café which bore her name. It was situated on Pacific Coast Highway close to Santa Monica; ironically, in a city where buildings are considered eminently disposable, the structure stood for some decades after Miss Todd had gone. In December 1935 she was discovered dead in her car, parked in the garage up the hill from her apartment. She was dressed in high film-star style – a mauve and silver evening gown and a $20,000 mink coat; her neck and wrists were covered with jewels.

At the inquest her death was ruled as being due to poisoning, but Mrs Wallace Ford, the actor's wife, said that she had been telephoned by Miss Todd twelve hours *after* she was supposed to have died ... and there were also reports of extortion threats against her. It is not far removed from the story of the blackmail of Mavis Weld – but, unlike that death, Thelma Todd's murder was never solved.

An astonishingly direct parallel between real life and one of Chandler's plots is that between the actual Dr George K. Dayley of Santa Monica and Dr Albert S. Almore in *The Lady in the Lake*. In February 1940, Dr Dayley, a respected physician, went on trial for the murder of his wife whose death, five years earlier, had been recorded as suicide. The prosecution alleged that Dr Dayley had drugged his wife, then carried her body to the garage where he placed her head near the car's exhaust pipe and then switched on the engine. Death was from carbon monoxide poisoning.

Over a hundred 'witnesses' testified against Dr Dayley, some saying that he had boasted of committing the perfect murder. No evidence was produced by the prosecution, however, to prove that Mrs Dayley had been drugged. After a four-day deliberation the jury failed to agree and Dr Dayley went free.

In *The Lady in the Lake* Dr Albert S. Almore of Bay City is suspect from his first appearance. Halfway through the story the reader learns that he specializes in giving morphine injections to patients who are 'hyper-tense'. His own wife commits suicide. How? By inhaling carbon monoxide fumes.... Later, the woman's parents allege that the doctor had previously injected her with a drug and carried her body into the garage. The novel was written only a year after the Dayley case and one would have thought that the similarities were so close as to be actionable.

In common with most of the United States, the incidence of crime in Los Angeles has risen several hundred per cent during the last two or three decades, and the amount of violent crime has increased in direct ratio. Of the seven major crimes in Los Angeles (homicide, rape, robbery, narcotics violations, aggravated assault, burglary, grand theft and auto theft), narcotics violations come top of the list. And it is people between seventeen and twenty years old who are the majority of the prosecuted offenders. It is this aspect of the increase which would be anathema to Marlowe: not so much the preponderance of trafficking in narcotics, prostitution and pornography which is immediately attendant upon the permissive society – drugs and their abuse feature frequently in Chandler's novels – but the very youthfulness of those who organize and those who fall victim to it. Marlowe's moral sense would be particularly outraged by the manipulation of the younger generation. As in the past, it is a middle-aged Mafia which promotes and controls the situation. Marlowe's opponents would be the same in the 1980s – even if the victims are scarcely out of school.

Chandler did not give Marlowe the opportunity to overmoralize, or to analyse, or to express an extended personal opinion on any subject; yet his feelings, his own (Chandler's) gritty, hard-boiled sense of values, do sometimes break surface even if only in a wise-crack. Marlowe's understanding of murder and murderers, his empiric reasoning from long experience, is given expression in a closing chapter of *The Long Goodbye*. It was one of the last, and possibly the best, of the novels to be written (1953) and Marlowe shows some softening. Chandler's wife, Cissy, was to die in 1954 after a long illness and Chandler may have been going through a particularly thoughtful period. Certainly this novel evinces a more philosophical, even romantic, view of human frailty. Marlowe does, in fact, call himself 'a romantic' and muses thus, exposing more of the inner man than at any time before:

> I got home late and tired and depressed. It was one of those nights when the air is heavy and the night noises seem muffled and far away. There was a high, misty indifferent moon. I walked the floor, played a few records and hardly heard them. I seemed to hear a steady ticking somewhere, but there wasn't anything in the house to tick. The ticking was in my head, I was a one-man death watch.
>
> I thought of the first time I had seen Eileen Wade and the second and the

third and the fourth. But after that something in her got out of drawing. She no longer seemed quite real. A murderer is always unreal once you know he is a murderer. There are people who kill out of hate or fear or greed. There are the cunning killers who plan and expect to get away with it. There are the angry killers who do not think at all. And there are the killers who are in love with death, to whom murder is a remote kind of suicide. In a sense they are all insane....

In Chandlertown the death watch goes on.

7
EROTIC AS A STALLION

Tinseltown, Whoretown, Sin City, Sex City – Chandlertown has had many, usually derogatory, names. They have derived, mostly, from the influence of Hollywood, the film factory: the meretricious gloss, the spurious glamour attracted tens – if not hundreds – of thousands with promises of fame and fortune. Amongst the established stars and the aspiring actors, the artists and the artisans, the business tycoons and the professional promoters, who settled in Los Angeles and its suburbs, and had genuine links with the industry, there also arrived the big racketeers and little crooks, the hucksters, hustlers, hookers and hoods. And if there was one exploitable commodity, one paramount element binding them all together, it was sex.

The movie business, of course, has always made the major contribution to what is, perhaps, a national obsession, and Chandlertown reveals the most concentrated expression of it. From Clara Bow, the original 'It' girl, to Jean Harlow and Jane Russell to Jayne Mansfield and Marilyn Monroe, the various sex goddesses were promoted not so much to stimulate the red corpuscles of the American male as to take the greenbacks from his pocket. The decline of the big Hollywood studios occurred in the late fifties. Sex exploitation, however, goes on.

There are very few moments when the reader sees Marlowe in a state of sexual excitement, but enough to realize that he was as susceptible to female charms as any all-American hero should be. In the earlier novels he is able to take it or leave it, wryly wise-cracking when some provocatively dressed, self-consciously attractive woman more or less throws herself at him:

> She hauled off and slapped me again, harder if anything. 'I think you'd better kiss me,' she breathed. Her eyes were clear and limpid and melting. I glanced down casually. Her right hand was balled into a very business-like fist. It wasn't too small to work with, either.
> 'Believe me,' I said. 'There's only one reason why I don't. Even if you had your little black gun with you. Or the brass knuckles you probably keep on your night table.'

She smiled politely.

'I might just happen to be working for you,' I said. 'And I don't go whoring around after every pair of legs I see.' I looked down at hers. I could see them all right and the flag that marked the goal line was no larger than it had to be. (*The Little Sister*)

That encounter was with Mavis Weld; Marlowe had it under control and did not allow the sexual invitation to deflect him from his investigative purposes. He liked 'class', that is style, not necessarily social rank, and would doubtless have taken opportunist advantage of a come-on if it were offered outside the line of duty – perhaps even *on* duty.

She slapped my wrist.
She said softly:
'What's your name?'
'Phil. What's yours?'
'Helen. Kiss me.'
She fell softly across my lap and I bent down over her face and began to browse on it. She worked her eyelashes and made butterfly kisses on my cheeks. When I got to her mouth it was half open and burning and her tongue was a darting snake between her teeth. (*Farewell, My Lovely*)

That was a rich society woman unperturbed when her husband opens the door a moment later and politely says, 'I beg your pardon.' Marlowe is unperturbed too. He knows these women are doublecrossers, two-timers, treacherous, dangerous – and therefore fair game.

In *The Long Goodbye* we get to see him somewhat hotter under the collar:

'Put me on the bed,' she breathed.
I did that. Putting my arms around her touched bare skin, soft skin, soft, yielding flesh. I lifted her and carried her the few steps to the bed and lowered her. She kept her arms around my neck. She was making some kind of whistling noise in her throat. Then she threshed about and moaned. This was murder. I was as erotic as a stallion. I was losing control. You don't get that sort of invitation from that sort of woman very often anywhere.

Well, opportunist Marlowe may be, but sex once again takes second place to duty. Later, though, he so far forgets himself, and his readers, as to contemplate marriage with another very rich woman in the story. He knows, despite all she tells him, that she does not love him. They sleep together and in the morning she says goodbye, leaving Marlowe with his own regrets.

We said goodbye. I watched the cab out of sight. I went back up the steps and into the bedroom and pulled the bed to pieces and remade it. There was a long dark hair on one of the pillows. There was a lump of lead at the pit of my stomach.... To say goodbye is to die a little.

Contemplating an empty, lonely future – as Chandler was himself at that time – Marlowe was in danger of becoming maudlin. It was the first time that the reader was permitted to know anything about the private life of this very private private eye, and it revealed him as both a realist and a romantic. For some it overstepped the bounds of the detective fiction formula: the sexy innuendo, the quick kiss following a slap across the mouth, was usually the limit of gumshoe–girl relationships. Actually to spend time describing them in bed together, let alone add romantic dialogue, was to hold up the action; only a writer like James M. Cain continually used lust as a motive for murder. But *The Long Goodbye* is a long novel, too, during which we get to know much more of Marlowe the man than in any of the preceding works. The next – and the last published – novel, *Playback*, was much shorter and shows Marlowe once more as a sexual opportunist, this time getting into bed with the girl he has been paid to follow. It is a scene more explicit in its description than any other.

> When I turned she was standing by the bed as naked as Aphrodite fresh from the Aegean. She stood there proudly without either shame or enticement.
> 'Damn it,' I said. 'When I was young you could undress a girl slowly. Nowadays she's in the bed while you're struggling with your collar button.'
> 'Well struggle with your goddam collar button.'
> She pulled the bedcovers back and lay on the bed shamelessly nude. She was just a beautiful naked woman completely unashamed of being what she was.

Later:

> I felt her tight and warm against me. Her body surged with vitality. Her beautiful arms held me tight. And again in the darkness that muted cry, and then again the slow quiet peace.
> 'I hate you,' she said, with her mouth against mine, 'not for this but because perfection never comes twice and with us it came too soon. And I'll never see you again and I don't want to. It would have to be for ever or not at all.'

Once again, it seems, Marlowe has missed out – found a bed-mate who could be more than just that too late. But the reader has had another glimpse of his behaviour as a lover – and into his emotional responses. At the very end of this, the last book in print, there comes an extraordinary romantic revelation. The case is concluded and once more Marlowe seems to be facing a future of bleak loneliness:

> I climbed the long flight of redwood steps and unlocked my door. Everything was the same. The room was stuffy and dull and impersonal as it always was. I opened a couple of windows and mixed a drink in the kitchen. Wherever I went, whatever I did, this was what I would come back to. A blank wall in a meaningless room in a meaningless house.

Then the telephone rings. It is Linda Loring, making an astonishing transmigration from *The Long Goodbye* to *Playback*. She is the rich woman who had suggested marriage in the earlier book. Now she proposes again, this time long-distance from Paris. 'How are you?' asks Marlowe.

> 'Lonely. Lonely for you, I've tried to forget you. I haven't been able to. We made beautiful love together.'
> 'That was a year and a half ago. And for one night. What am I supposed to say?'
> 'I've been faithful to you. I don't know why. The world is full of men. But I've been faithful to you.'
> 'I haven't been faithful to you, Linda. I didn't think I'd ever see you again. I didn't know you expected me to be faithful.'

Such dialogue would have been unthinkable in, say, *The Big Sleep* or *Farewell, My Lovely*. When Linda pleads with Marlowe to reconsider marriage and offers to send him a plane ticket to Paris, he is outraged at such an insult to his manly independence and says he will send *her* a plane ticket. We are left with the future unresolved. 'I'll be here. I always am,' says Marlowe, and is left by his creator awaiting marriage to Linda. Chandler's last work, *The Poodle Springs Story* (Palm Springs, that is) was unfinished when he died, but in the first two chapters* Marlowe has been married to Linda for 'just three weeks and four days'.

The dialogue is full of embarrassingly arch references to their sexual relationship and one cannot help feeling that the novel, had it been finished, would have been something of a disappointment. Chandler had misgivings about the marriage, if not the novel:

> PS. I am writing him married to a rich woman and swamped by money, but I don't think it will last.†

Be that as it may, the progressive intrusion of sex in *The Long Goodbye* and *Playback*, the increasingly overt descriptions, Marlowe's apparent disapproval of the forwardness of women in the bedroom, point towards the sexual obsessiveness of Chandlertown today. Chandler reflected it, perhaps unconsciously, in Marlowe's changing attitude. Marlowe could see it – sensed it – coming, so he would hardly be surprised by the pornographic bookshops and cinemas which have sprung up all over Los Angeles, sometimes whole blocks of them.

*Published in *Raymond Chandler Speaking*
†From a letter to Maurice Guinness, in *Raymond Chandler Speaking*.

Pornography, as Chandler fans know, was an ingredient of the first Marlowe novel, *The Big Sleep*. Mr Arthur Gwynn Geiger runs a bookshop – 'Rare Books and De Luxe Editions' – on what is, from Chandler's descriptions, obviously Hollywood Boulevard; the shop is a front for a pornographic lending library. Marlowe follows a client 'across Highland', west for another block, then turns right, then left again, which would bring him onto Franklyn Avenue where, in the same book, Marlowe's office is situated. (In *The Little Sister* Franklyn Avenue is also the location for a gang killing.) It is an area that Marlowe knows well. There were, and still are, two or three most reputable bookshops on Hollywood Boulevard. Marlowe enters one of them, opposite Geiger's, for information. He also does a little research in the Hollywood Public Library on Ivar, a few blocks away. Today the library is still there with its thirties decor intact just as Chandler knew it. Right next door is a porn bookshop and a nude review offering the 'indescribable filth' that Geiger's clients had to obtain so clandestinely – although, of course, *their* books were 'well bound, handsomely printed in handset type on fine paper', not the mass-produced and often illiterate paperbacks and magazines which make up most of today's avalanche of erotica.

More than 60 per cent of all pornographic literature available in the United States is produced in California, and Chandlertown is the biggest and most immediate outlet for it. The market is so vast that it represents really big business – and big profits: estimates put the turnover figure above $5000 million dollars.

Farther east from the Hollywood Public Library, where the neighbourhoods get somewhat seedier even than Hollywood itself, on Hollywood Boulevard, on Sunset, on Santa Monica, on Melrose, on Beverly, all of which run parallel east–west, and on some of the main north–south routes – Western, Normandie, Vermont, Hoover – there are entire blocks of porn shops selling not only graphically illustrated literature but sex aids such as vibrators, dildos, huge rubber dolls of both sexes, slides, films and sadomasochistic equipment. It is all part of a huge sex industry, most of it run by criminal syndicates with which Marlowe would today inevitably find himself entangled. Apart from the porn shops, there are a large number of porn cinemas showing every conceivable sort of blue film – heterosexual and homosexual – round the clock. At one recent twenty-four-hour 'festival' of gay porn films, customers were advised to bring their own 'bedding and booze'. Other cinemas advertise 'cruise loops', that is, places where the audience may not only pick each other up but exercise the libido in a more direct way....

In modern Chandlertown it is not only two-dimensional fantasy sex

In The Big Sleep *Marlowe goes to the Hollywood Pubic Library on Ivar to do a little research. The building still stands today, totally unchanged*

that is on offer; the real thing is there for the asking – and the paying: go-go girls, go-go boys, simulated and actual sex acts performed for entertainment, as well as regular establishments of prostitution.

The sex which Marlowe occasionally enjoyed and which was discreetly available for his rich clients is now a part of Los Angeles living on a scale which would leave him as stunned as if he had been sapped.

In the early seventies the *Los Angeles Times* published a whole supplement on 'obscenity'. On the front page there appeared a nice, clean, all-American family – Mom, Pop, elder brother and two kid sisters. In heavy black type beneath were the words 'THEY ARE UNDER

ATTACK', together with a splash of red ink, presumably representing bloodstains.

Despite being entitled a 'report', the supplement was a rather tendentious tract endeavouring to equate psychopathic murders with pornography. There were emotive drawings – a policeman bending over the blanket-covered body of a child lying on a stretcher; a fresh-faced young schoolgirl being solicited by a sinister-looking man in a cruising car – as well as wholly unsubstantiated statements linking mass murder with the reading of obscene material.

Pavlov's experiments on the conditioned response in dogs were held to parallel the stimulating effect that pornography could have on 'ordinary, decent people' (whoever and wherever they may be), and there were solemn quotes on vice, goodness and moral cleanliness from such an unlikely assortment of bedfellows as Alexander Pope, Alexis de Tocqueville and Loretta Young.

Whether the apparently susceptible citizens of Los Angeles were saved from *moral* degradation by the 'report' is impossible to tell; certainly it in no way lessened the flood of pornographic material found throughout the city. Morals apart, the crime wave continued to increase.

It is not only spilled blood which disfigures the Los Angeles streets as a result of the porn industry. More apparent are the garish advertisements, the crudely painted establishments, which turn an otherwise unremarkable if rundown neighbourhood into a lurid semblance of honky-tonk town. Violent colours, blatant signs, amateurishly executed pictures attempt to lure the passerby into whatever form of fantasy sex he or she seeks.

In *The Big Sleep* Marlowe meets a shady insurance broker who has an office in the Fulwider Building, Western and Santa Monica. If the area was less than elegant thirty odd years ago, today – apart from a couple of small branch banks on the corner – the junction of Western and Santa Monica is characterized by a rash of massage parlours, nude girl exhibitions, pornographic bookshops, sex cinemas and cheap snack bars used for quick pick-ups. Police patrol cars are more or less constantly in evidence, tough-looking hoods dodge in and out of the doorways, collecting dues from prostitutes who solicit from just inside the shop frcnts. It is reminiscent of this brief description from a pre-Marlowe short story, 'Pick-Up on Noon Street':

> The car slid along Los Angeles to Fifth, east to San Pedro, south again for block after block, quiet blocks and loud blocks, blocks where silent men sat on

shaky front porches and blocks where noisy young toughs of both colours snarled and wise-cracked at one another in front of cheap restaurants and drugstores and beer-parlours full of slot machines.

If Prohibition was the impetus in the Chandlertown of the twenties and thirties, then the quest for sex, fed by pornography, is the equivalent today. *Plus ça change....*

8
PUNCH DRUNK BY THIS TIME

Philip Marlowe was a man's man. Well built, athletic, hard, self-sufficient, courageous, undemonstrative, taciturn, conservative, he would have been almost as at home in an English pub as in an American bar. Not quite, of course. Chandler's years at Dulwich College and his short term at the Admiralty gave him a respect for English education and certain British institutions, but as a young man (in his later years he came to revere British social customs rather more) he was irked by the formality of English society, by its class consciousness, its hypocrisy; in that he was wholly American and this was directly reflected in the behaviour and reactions of Philip Marlowe.

As an ex-cop turned private eye, Marlowe was constantly in touch with the worst that mankind could produce and this naturally created his veneer of world-weary cynicism. Not only the real reservoirs of evil, the big-time racketeers, the thieves and murderers, and the people who used them to do their dirty work, but the minor crooks, not so much desperadoes as those desperate to escape from the wretchedness of the lower echelons of American society. For such losers Marlowe had some sympathy, as he had for anyone who retained vestiges of pride or pluck even though his morals might have slipped a little. Marlowe's own morals were not so likely to slip as to get pushed. His basic puritanism never changed, but if he had to cover for a client or for someone in a jam while he got at the final truth, he was not above failing to report a crime, even if that crime was murder.

In a less fundamental way, Marlowe's fastidiousness is frequently revealed in his reaction to small personal traits: to flamboyance in dress, to an over-particular personal toilet or its reverse, a lack of personal hygiene. All the period prejudices are there: men wearing suede shoes, silk scarves, carefully arranged pocket handkerchiefs, jewellery, cologne. Men with carefully manicured nails were as distasteful as men with nails bitten down; fatness, baldness, bad teeth and bad breath were all characteristics reserved for the bad guys. Clammy hands seemed to be the ultimate Chandler detestation: even in pre-Marlowe days he has his private eye, John Dalmas, reacting thus:

> He came over and held out his hand. I shook it. It was as clammy as a dead fish. Clammy hands and the people who own them make me sick. ('Red Wind')

The clammy hand in question belonged to Copernik, a big, brutal cop who was not above a bit of cover-up himself; he had halitosis, too.

But on the whole Marlowe respected cops. They were human beings, open to corruption, but in the main they got Marlowe's grudging approval. Physical toughness was a quality which more than compensated for character defects. A man who could handle himself in a fight, who could take a beating and bounce back with his bare fists, was calculated to get the reader's sympathy as well as Marlowe's. He was himself that sort of man.

> His face froze and he swung his arm back to slug me [with the barrel of a gun] a third time with the power behind it. His arm was still going back when I took a half step forward and kicked him in the pit of the stomach.
> I didn't think, I didn't plan, I didn't figure my chances or whether I had any. I just got enough of his yap and I ached and bled and maybe I was just a little punch drunk by this time.
> He jack-knifed, gasping, and the gun fell out of his hand. He groped for it wildly, making strained sounds deep in his throat. I put a knee into his face. He screeched. (*The Long Goodbye*)

Not Queensberry rules, of course, but all good clean fun between tough guys. Marlowe was enough of a realist to employ the kick in the stomach, the knee in the groin, during his more 'hand to hand' moments. Such action is not only part of the traditional repertoire of the private investigator but of the wider American obsession with the he-man. Chandler seemed to have little professional respect for Ernest Hemingway. 'Who is this Hemingway person at all?' asks a puzzled and exasperated cop. 'A guy that keeps saying the same thing over and over until you believe it must be good,' is Marlowe's answer. Nevertheless, Hemingway's own preoccupation with virile masculinity found a parallel in Chandler–Marlowe, and while it is a nationwide syndrome, it finds most of its most overt expression in Chandlertown – once more through the influence of Hollywood. At the time of writing current box-office male stars are men who have cultivated the tough-guy image – Brando, Newman, Eastwood, Bronson, Reynolds, Caan, Stallone – they continue a long line of American heroes who have specialized in physical toughness. Only a handful – Beatty, Redford, Nicholson – have sought a wider range, and even they have had to serve a bare-knuckle, gun-toting apprenticeship before graduating to roles of greater complexity.

In the agents' offices, at cocktail parties, at poolside barbecues, on the beach, in the ball park, it is still the beefcake image which predominates in Los Angeles – or at least, the one which most men under middle age aim at. It may be more athletic than aggressive, but even when the flesh is failing (business executives burdened with expense-account bellies are to be seen in droves jogging up and down the quieter residential streets in a last effort to maintain the muscles), this physical style still indicates unflagging virility: 'machismo' is a favourite word in conversations, in articles and in advertising copy aimed at men. Marlowe always recognized machismo when he saw it and it has continued down the decades as the main ingredient of the big, outdoor, Californian image, despite the general emasculation achieved by what is, in reality, a matriarchal society. Sheer size is part of the machismo mystique. Not synonymous with honesty, of course, but usually deserving some grudging respect, even when the big guy is a murderer. In *Farewell, My Lovely*, besides the big dumb cop Hemingway, there is the biggest Chandler character of them all, the ex-con Moose Malloy, looking for his two-timing Velma. Malloy's huge size is presented for our admiration; he is a basically gentle, soft-voiced, sad-eyed giant who doesn't know his own strength, a killer by accident rather than compulsion, besotted with the double-crossing dame who finally shoots him. He is the big, archetypal fall guy, Samson brought low by Delilah.

In the same book there is yet another giant, a beachcomber with a boat, girlish-faced but tough, an ex-cop like Marlowe, full of cynical wisdom with which to back the physical power which Marlowe so admires:

> I looked at him again. He had the eyes you never see, that you only read about. Violet eyes. Almost purple. Eyes like a girl, a lovely girl. His skin was as soft as silk. Lightly reddened, but it would never tan. It was too delicate. He was bigger than Hemingway and younger, by many years. He was not as big as Moose Malloy, but he looked very fast on his feet. His hair was that shade of red that glints with gold. But except for the eyes he had a plain farmer face, with no stagey kind of handsomeness.

From that description one could be forgiven for thinking that Marlowe was bi-sexual, if not an outright homosexual. There are other instances throughout the novels where the appraisal of a man's physical attractiveness could be misconstrued. But Marlowe, like Chandler, hated queers. Whenever they appear – and it is surprising, considering the dates of some of the works in which they do, that the descriptions and the inferences are so open – they are either the usual overdressed scented queens or else homicidal psychopaths. Marlowe's contempt for them is manifest.

> The door opened silently and I was looking at a tall, blond man in a white flannel suit with a violet satin scarf around his neck.

There was a cornflower in the lapel of his white coat and his pale blue eyes looked faded out by comparison. The violet scarf was loose enough to show that he wore no tie and that he had a thick, soft brown neck, like the neck of a strong woman. His features were a little on the heavy side, but handsome, he had an inch of height more than I had, which made him six foot one. His blond hair was arranged, by art or nature, in three precise blond ledges which reminded me of steps, so that I didn't like them. I wouldn't have liked them anyway. Apart from all this he had the general appearance of a lad who would wear a white flannel suit with a violet scarf round his neck and a cornflower in his lapel. (*Farewell, My Lovely*)

Even his size could not diffuse Marlowe's dislike for this specimen upon whom he later smelled perfume!

In the same book a queer makes a brief, typical appearance as a pianist-crooner in a bar; he is there merely as an adjunct to the scene, a cheap restaurant where the food is bad:

A male cutie with henna'd hair drooped at a bungalow grand piano and tickled the keys lasciviously and sang 'Stairway to the Stars' in a voice with half the steps missing.

In *The Big Sleep* the pornographic bookshop owner, Geiger, is a homosexual who keeps a tough young man, Carol Lundgren, as a lover. When Geiger is murdered, Lundgren lays out Geiger's body with elaborate oriental ritual, then shoots the man who he thinks is responsible for the killing. Marlowe catches him and together they return to Geiger's house:

'Alright,' I said. 'You have a key. Let's go in.'
'Who said I had a key?'
'Don't kid me, son. The fag gave you one. You've got a nice, clean, manly little room in there. He shooed you out and locked it up when he had lady visitors. He was like Caesar, a husband to women and a wife to men. Think I can't figure people like him and you out?'
I still had his automatic more or less pointed at him, but he swung on me just the same. It caught me flush on the chin. I backstepped fast enough to keep from falling, but I took plenty of the punch. It was meant to be a hard one, but a pansy has no iron in his bones, whatever he looks like.

Marlowe's prejudiced generalization would, today, perhaps only bother the most militant member of Gay Lib, but the extraordinary outburst by Roger Wade, an alcoholic author in *The Long Goodbye*, must represent Chandler's own feelings of resentment against both homosexuals and, somewhat astonishingly, critics; the fact that the book was published in 1953 reflects the fact that homosexuals were, by then, beginning to come out of their closets.

'You know something?' he asked suddenly and his voice suddenly seemed much more clear. 'I had a male secretary once. Used to dictate to him. Let him go. Mistake. Ought to have kept him. Word would have got around that I was a homo. The clever boys that write book reviews because they can't write anything else would have caught on and started giving me the build-up. Have to take care of their own, you know. They're all queers, every damn one of them. The queer is the artistic arbiter of our age, chum. The pervert is the top guy, now.'

Thirty years later Wade would find much more to shout about. Together with New York and San Francisco, Los Angeles has become – even more than the other cities, perhaps – the home of homosexuals in huge numbers. All types of queer - butch and bitch, elegant and casual, rough and refined, straight and kinky – live openly 'devious' lives in every sort of neighbourhood, scoring in the streets and parks and on the beaches, making out in bars and baths, cruising in the cinemas, catered for by commerce and even the Church,* in a way that Wade would think indicates that not only are they the 'artistic arbiters' of the age, but arbiters in every other aspect of life as well, from politics to economics, from science to sport. And why not? A person's sexual proclivities are, in the main, irrelevant to their position within, and their contribution to, the society of which they are a part.

Most homosexuals in Chandlertown arrived there because of the magnet of the movies. Wade's generalization *was* partly right: it *is* a fairly accurate assessment that the arts attract a more-than-average number of homosexuals whose talents are manifested in something creative, and the movie industry, apart from acting, writing, composing and directing, has its attendant demands for cosmeticians, hair dressers, decorators and designers, many of whom, by some not-easily-definable sociogenetic chemistry, happen to be homosexual.

On the other hand (and this is the result of empiric observation; a Kinsey is needed for factual analysis), thousands, and even tens of thousands, of gay people in Los Angeles are employed in jobs not remotely connected with the arts. In the revolution of recognition which has happened since Marlowe's day, it was the artistic queers who were first able to build a bridgehead to general acceptance; the others, in more mundane employment, no longer need the elaborate processes of cover-up after that initial success.

These days, however, in a straight fight (if that is not a contradiction in terms!) Marlowe might have to eat his words about a pansy having

---

*See the Rev. Troy Perry's book *The Lord is My Shepherd and He Knows I'm Gay*, Nash Publishing Corporation, 1972.

no 'iron in his bones'. Even 'male cuties' can turn out to be tough cookies, as the contemporary Los Angeles Police Force knows.

Marlowe did not have to establish his heterosexuality; it was taken for granted. His friendship and affection for Terry Lennox in *The Long Goodbye* could remain unquestioned as straightforward, instinctive comradeship, a buddy relationship in which Marlowe could – out of some sense of purely masculine affinity – put himself at considerable risk. In the same book Marlowe considered marriage. It was the combination of affection for both sexes that some readers and several critics thought to be untypically sentimental. Maybe Marlowe was growing up, becoming a three-dimensional human being instead of a hero-cipher. At least (and at last) we have a glimpse of the sort of man he admired when he said: 'Terry Lennox was my friend. I've got a reasonable amount of sentiment invested in him.'

9
WOMEN MAKE ME SICK

If Marlowe was a man's man, he was also, in today's overused idiom, a male chauvinist. In contemporary Chandlertown he would be in good company. In spite of the new liberalism, old attitudes die extremely hard.

Marlowe's response to women was unequivocal, in the mainstream of man's traditional assumption that the female was put by God upon the earth to breed, to run a home, to cook, sew and, occasionally seduce. Thus she was and is often seen as weak, guileful, shallow, avaricious, treacherous, pretty – and a plaything who can easily wreck a man's life.

Marlowe ran across some of the worst specimens of this species, irrespective of their age or social standing; their greed and vanity are the recurring themes that either directly or indirectly motivate murder. They were the gold-diggers, social climbers, nymphomaniacs, psychopaths, monstrous matriarchs, slatternly degenerates.

To men they were up for grabs, open to opportunism, to be manipulated, manoeuvred, used, pampered, spoilt, cosseted, but never really loved or cherished in the way that Chandler himself loved and cherished Cissy. Illusion and disillusion were the repeated, contrapuntal themes which the good guys and the bad guys reiterated to each other.

The bed was down. Something in it giggled. A blonde head was pressed into my pillow. Two bare arms curved up and the hands belonging to them were clasped on top of the blonde head. Carmen Sternwood lay on her back, in my bed, giggling at me. The tawny wave of her hair was spread out on the pillow as if by a careful and artificial hand. Her slaty eyes peered at me, and had the effect, as usual, of peering from behind a barrel. She smiled. Her small sharp teeth glinted.
'Cute, aren't I?' she said. (*The Big Sleep*)

Carmen Sternwood, the murderous, man-crazy daughter of the rich general, makes her play for Marlowe. So does her married sister, Vivian Regan, protective, but scarcely more moral.

'Move closer,' she said almost thickly.

I moved out from under the wheel into the middle of the seat. She turned her body a little away from me as if to peer out of the window. Then she let herself fall backwards, without a sound, into my arms. Her head almost struck the wheel. Her eyes were closed, her face was dim. Then I saw that her eyes opened and flickered, the shine of them visible even in the darkness.

'Hold me close, you beast,' she said.

I put my arms round her loosely at first. Her hair had a harsh feeling against my face. I tightened my arms and lifted her up. I brought her face slowly up to my face. Her eyelids were flickering rapidly, like moth wings.

I kissed her lightly and quickly. Then a long slow clinging kiss. Her lips opened under mine. Her body began to shake in my arms.

'Killer,' she said softly, her breath going into my mouth.

I strained her to me until the shivering of her body was almost shaking mine. I kept on kissing her. After a long time she pulled her head far enough away to say: 'Where do you live?' (*The Big Sleep*)

Where Marlowe lives is as usual pinpointed geographically, and in the end he doesn't take her there; he takes her home instead.

The Sternwood daughters are a vicious pair, and a rather pathetic gangster's moll makes a trio – their collective immorality unrelieved by any other female in the book except, perhaps, the smart but only quietly sexy assistant in the bookshop opposite Geiger's. Indeed, the only other woman of any consequence is the girlfriend of a blackmailer, who finally made her getaway by selling some information for a couple of hundred bucks, not vicious but venal, and as worthless as the others; worth even less, in fact, a mere two hundred dollars.

In *Farewell, My Lovely* the elusive chorus girl Velma turned out to be the adulterous socialite who murdered twice before committing suicide. In the same book, Ann Riordan is one of the few, if not the only, girls in the Chandler canon with moral principles, and she is a cop's daughter. Chandler gives her a very detailed description:

She was about twenty-eight years old. She had a rather narrow forehead of more height than is considered elegant. Her nose was small and inquisitive, her upper lip a shade too long and her mouth more than a shade too wide. Her eyes were grey-blue with flecks of gold in them. She had a nice smile. It was a nice face, a face you get to like. Pretty, but not so pretty that you would have to wear brass knuckles every time you took it out.

She was pert, sharp, independent, and a self-appointed assistant to Marlowe. Throughout the book she angled for his closer attentions, invited him to use her spare room when he turned up having been beaten up, and became angry when he refused. His motivation in refusing was not obvious; maybe he wanted to recover in privacy, more likely he could see the marital hook dangling on the line. Hadn't he himself said to her: 'A fellow could settle down here. Move right in. Everything set for him.' Later, after he had decided to leave, he observed to himself, 'It would be a nice room to wear slippers in.' Back in his apartment he realized that he had done the right thing.

> I unlocked the door of my apartment and went in and sniffed the smell of it, just standing there, against the door for a little while before I put the light on. A homely smell, a smell of dust and tobacco smoke, the smell of a world where men live, and keep on living.

It had been a narrow escape for this man's man, Philip Marlowe, and by the end of the book, when Ann Riordan makes her last appearance, we know the danger has passed. Structurally she was a necessity – Marlowe had to explain to her (and the readers) some of the missing details in the detective work. In female fashion she ends the scene with the line: 'I'd like to be kissed, damn you.' Did Marlowe oblige? We are never given the opportunity to know. In the last published story in which Marlowe appears, 'The Pencil', he once more meets Ann Riordan and once again he makes use of her and her apartment:

> 'I need your help,' I said.
> 'That's the only time I ever see you.'

Ann Riordan's answer reveals much. She was a threat because she was too suitable: pretty, intelligent, brave, the closest Chandler ever got to endowing a woman with basic integrity. Marlowe's attitude to women is perhaps succinctly summed up in *The Big Sleep*.

> I went out to the kitchenette and drank two cups of black coffee. You can have a hangover from other things than alcohol. I had one from women. Women made me sick.

From the security of an idyllic marriage, Chandler could vilify his fictional women, endow them with the dangerous attributes and weaknesses that have accrued to the sex since Shakespeare wrote 'Frailty, thy name is woman!' It is an attitude of mind which, despite the manifest and manifold advances of Women's Lib, still reveals itself in thousands of Los Angeles barroom conversations. In Chandlertown the war of the sexes continues to be fought with a vicious savagery. Two examples, gratuitously presented while I was collecting material for this book, will serve to indicate the general antipathy towards women in a town which continues to exploit them. A young graduate, working in a writers' agency in Hollywood, recently gave his views on marriage. Not for him, he said. There were only two reasons he would contemplate it. One, if the girl were 'really loaded', the other if his professional success necessitated it.

'Why marry?' he asked. 'Hollywood is full of chicks waiting to be laid – why marry?' A sexually useful liaison was his only interest in women. If he did eventually form a legal union, he said, he'd have to have a penthouse in some fairly anonymous apartment block (Century City was his ideal) where he could go when he 'got lucky'.

Way up in the success scale (the heights to which the youthful agent presumably aspired) the same attitude was revealed by a millionaire magnate with business interests in several Los Angeles industries – films, pop music, aerospace, electronics. Still only in his forties, he has been twice married and twice divorced, and is always in the company of some beautiful, expensively dressed young woman – real Marlowe 'cuties' all – about whom he will subsequently talk with cruel candour, using them as examples to reinforce his dyspeptic misogynist opinions, how 'all women are whores' (a favourite aphorism), how impossible it is to find a really good, loving, faithful woman, how the only thing to do is to 'use them and throw them away like paper cups' – and to 'have a good lawyer'.

The women are capable of being equally contemptuous. 'I'll do anything with any man so long as he's rich enough,' one attractive girl – the 'friend' of a film producer – said. 'I'll go along with his kinks, I'll play dumb or smart, whichever way he wants it so long as I get my hands on real money.'

Dumb or smart, Chandler's women were usually clothes conscious, using this for predatory purposes.

> She stood there half-smiling, in the high-necked white fox evening coat she had told me about. Emerald pendants hung from her ears and almost buried themselves in the soft white fur. (*Farewell, My Lovely*)

The white fox and sparklers of the deadly Mrs Grayle – literally got up to kill – were almost *de rigueur* for a forties *femme fatale*.

> Her hair was fluffed out carelessly and she hadn't bothered with make-up. She wore a hostess gown and very little else. Her legs ended in little green and silver slippers. (*The Little Sister*)

Exactly the sort of thing a film star (Mavis Weld) might wear when you called on her unexpectedly – she was supposed to have been in her bath. Her companion, Dolores, with heavy Spanish accent, favoured lots of dramatic black with occasional touches of red.

> She was all in black, like the night before, but a tailor-made outfit this time, a wide black straw hat set at a rakish angle, the collar of a white silk shirt folded out over the collar of her jacket, and her throat bare and supple and her mouth as red as a new fire engine.

71

Red lips and nails were frequently noted details, and of course they have remained a fairly constant conceit over the last thirty years or more. In Hollywood the furs, the satins, the close-fitting, slinky gowns, the lounge pyjamas (which frequently appeared in the Chandler short stories) of the thirties and forties, the Jean Harlow image if you will, have remained a uniform for seduction, whatever the current dictates of Paris, Rome, London or New York.

On Hollywood Boulevard and on Santa Monica Boulevard there are several shops which cater for the *femme fatale*, displaying gowns (the very word is dated) which would have dressed any Chandler female (it would be inaccurate to call them heroines): black sequins and silver lamé, velvet trimmed with maribou, silk enriched with fur, the shape more or less unchanging – figure-fitting, low cut front and back. It is part of Hollywood's perpetuation of the archetypal glamorous female, seemingly for ever dressed either for cocktails or a dinner date. Indeed, such prototypes can be seen like an overblown, overgrown archipelago amidst a sea of denim, even amongst the mid-morning supermarket shoppers.

Just how much Raymond Chandler's work helps to continue this curiously idealized image is difficult to say. Without doubt the deliberate resuscitation of the fashion via remakes of the Chandler films – including the recent *Farewell, My Lovely* and the deliberate pastiche, *Chinatown* – created a new, if short-lived, revival of the vogue. Sartorial fashions are cyclical, but there is no question that silk and satin revivals are also the stylistic antidote to the ubiquitous blue jeans. It is a natural transition from the hippy cheesecloth of the sixties to the polysynthetic satins of the eighties, from the new new-frontierswomen to the new *femmes fatales* who have always existed side by side in American society. Marlowe just ran into the latter more often.

He would perhaps be dismayed by today's emancipation of women, their preponderance in positions of importance in business, in politics, in the arts (not that Marlowe was very interested in the arts except when he is used as a mouthpiece for his creator's literary opinions and

---

Above right: *In* The Big Sleep *Marlowe says he was 'dropped off in Hollywood near the Chinese Theatre'. This cinema is one of the few in Hollywood that has preserved its original architectural fantasy. It is famous, of course, for the array of film star signatures written in the concrete of the forecourt*

Right: *Hollywood Boulevard has lost much of the elegance it had in the thirties but it still contains some excellent Art-Deco shopfronts of the period*

prejudices – occasionally he makes reference to good music) and in civic life. But Chandlertown has always been full of independent women. Whether they stem from all those intrepid homesteaders trekking across the deserts and mountains throughout the nineteenth century only a social anthropologist could say, but of all the big, sophisticated American cities, Los Angeles seems to have a bigger share of self-reliant dames. This must be partly due to geography. Chandlertown is an outdoor town: girls go swimming and surfing alone in the deceptively misnamed Pacific Ocean, with its huge waves and treacherous undertow; housewives drive scores of miles on the terrifying freeways just to go shopping or deliver the kids to school or a party (no other urban housewife anywhere in the world *needs* to drive so far or so often); they sail their dinghies single-handed, ride horses in the surrounding hills, go trekking and camping and skiing in the mountains. For years – long before the movement for womens liberation was underway – they have done all those things on their own terms, the men going along as partners, not as automatic leaders, and for two decades the various modern movements – the beatniks, the hippies, the dropouts from every social class – have consolidated the sexual, social, professional independence of the 'weaker' sex. Paradoxically, it has also cemented the old opinions, widened the gulf, confirmed the prejudices that Marlowe held. Many of the men in Chandlertown will still say that women are essentially weak, guileful, shallow, avaricious, treacherous, pretty playthings. . . .

10
A FLESH-PINK MERCEDES-BENZ

Chandlertown is the world's greatest example of the automotive society: a huge metropolitan area – or rather, a series of urban communities – linked by elaborate networks of roads. During the last two decades a vast web of freeways has been superimposed upon the basic grid plan. They were only just beginning to be built in Marlowe's day:

> A traffic light not working, a boulevard stop or two, the entrance to the Freeway. There was plenty of traffic on it even at midnight. California's loaded with people going places and making speed to get there. If you don't drive eighty miles an hour, everybody passes you. If you do, you have to watch the rear-view mirror for highway patrol cars. It's the rat race of rat races. ('The Pencil')

The eighties have not brought many changes. Despite the reduced speed limit (50 m.p.h.) imposed since the oil crisis, much of the freeway traffic travels at least ten miles per hour above the legal limit; and that is taking into account the fact that most Angelinos are highly disciplined drivers (there is very little of the competitive driving so common in Europe) and that the freeways are heavily patrolled by motorcycle cops, squad cars and police helicopters.

The freeways are still 'loaded with people going places', even during the small hours of the night. The volume of traffic on, say, the San Diego freeway, or the Ventura freeway, or the Santa Ana freeway, or the Santa Monica freeway, or the Hollywood freeway, or the San Bernadino freeway, or the Pomona freeway, or the Longbeach freeway, is astounding. Where are all these people going at the dead of night? Not just great transcontinental trucks, oil tankers and container wagons, but thousands of private sedans, sports cars, mini-buses, souped-up panel trucks and pick-ups, buggies and motorcycles, all rushing through the night from the edge of the ocean to the edge of the desert, across the Hollywood Hills to the San Fernando valley, uptown, downtown, great restless rivers of light, white headlights and ruby-red tail lights, bearing the citizens of Chandlertown on an endless quest. But for what? Maybe just the frenetic need for movement itself, getting high on the highways.

Even before the freeways there was a constant movement along the city's arteries:

> I drove east on Sunset but I didn't go home. At La Brea I turned north and swung over to Highland, out over Cahuenga pass and down on to Ventura Boulevard, past Studio City and Sherman Oaks and Encino. There was nothing lonely about the trip. There never is on that road. Fast boys in stripped-down Fords shot in and out of the traffic streams, missing fenders by a sixteenth of an inch, but somehow always missing them. Tired men in dusty coupés and sedans winced and tightened their grip on the wheel and ploughed on north and west towards home and dinner, an evening with the sports page, the bleating of the radio, the whining of their spoiled children and the gabble of their silly wives.... Great double trucks rumbled down over Sepulveda from Wilmington and San Pedro and crossed towards the Ridge Route, starting up in low from the traffic lights with a growl of lions in the zoo.... I drove on to the Oxnard cut-off and turned back along the ocean. The big eight-wheelers and sixteen-wheelers were streaming north and hung over with orange lights. (*The Little Sister*)

Chandler does not explain why Marlowe drives that long circuitous route, mixing with the tired commuters and the heavy commercial traffic; he knew his readers would understand Marlowe's restlessness, how driving around was a common means of clearing the mind, calming the nerves, easing the tension, rather than simply a matter of getting from A to B.

In the late 1950s the great inter-state highways were being built and in the last published novel, *Playback* (1958), Marlowe makes use of the new stretch of highway running south from Los Angeles towards San Diego (down to 'Esmerelda' where much of the action takes place, a small town based on La Jolla where Chandler had settled):

> I left Los Angeles and hit the super highway that now by-passed Oceanside. I had time to think.
>
> From San Onofre to Oceanside were eighteen miles of divided six-lane super-highway dotted at intervals with the carcasses of wrecked, stripped and abandoned cars tossed against the high bank to rust until they were hauled away.

The whole American continent, from the Atlantic to the Pacific, from the Canadian to the Mexican border, is scattered with the remains of the metal dinosaurs from Detroit, but the freeways encircling Chandlertown are nowadays free of debris and well landscaped, the embankments covered with grass and ivy, oleander and plumbago. Public transport is poor, but the Los Angeles freeways are one of the great engineering achievements of the century, affording mobility to all but the poorest citizens.

It is the car, in fact, that is the greatest status symbol in Chandlertown. The need to be mobile means that the almost one-to-one ratio of people to cars allows everybody to express his individuality by what he drives. It is a surer mark of character and social standing than a man's house or his clothes, especially amongst the non-conformist young who are prepared to wear the ubiquitous blue-jean uniform but reveal their personalities in every type of vehicle, from extraordinary motorcycles and tricycles to custom-built monsters costing thousands of dollars and almost worthy of the appellation pop art.

Chandler was nearly always specific about cars, never content to write about just a sedan or a coupé, but usually naming the make and the model:

I reached a flash out of my pocket and went down grade and looked at the car. It was a Packard convertible, maroon or dark brown. (*The Big Sleep*)

The car was a dark blue seven-passenger sedan, a Packard of the latest model, custom-built. (*Farewell, My Lovely*)

Outside stood two Cadillacs, a Lincoln Continental and a Packard Clipper. Neither of the Cadillacs had the right colour or licence. Across the way a guy in riding breeches was sprawled with his legs over the door of a low-cut Lancia. (*The Little Sister*)

The first time I laid eyes on Terry Lennox he was drunk in a Rolls-Royce Silver Wraith outside the terrace of the Dancers. (*The Long Goodbye*)

'I want the licence number of Mrs Leslie Murdock's car.'
'It's 2X1111, a grey Mercury Convertible, 1940 model.' (*The High Window*)

A neat black Cadillac coupé came out of the garage. (*The Lady in the Lake*)

A couple of dozen cars, no more. I looked them over. One hunch at least had paid off. The Buick Roadmaster solid top bore a licence number I had in my pocket. It was parked almost at the entrance and next to it in the very last space near the entrance was a pale green and ivory Cadillac convertible with oyster white leather seats, a plaid travelling rug thrown over the front seat to keep it dry and all the gadgets a dealer could think of, including two enormous spot lights with mirrors on them, a radio aerial almost long enough for a tuna boat, a folding chromium luggage rack to help out the boot if you wanted to travel far and in style, a sun visor, a prism reflector to pick up traffic lights obscured by the visor, a radio with enough knobs on it for a control panel, a cigarette lighter into which you dropped your cigarette and it smoked it for you, and various other trifles which made me wonder how long it would be before they installed radar, sound-recording equipment, a bar and an anti-aircraft battery. (*Playback*)

77

Chandler was anticipating, almost by a decade, the gadget gimmickry of James Bond's Aston Martin.

Snobbery, of course, has always provided a place for expensive foreign automobiles in Chandlertown, beginning perhaps with the rise of the movie industry and the need of the great stars to display their status. The cars were as symbolic of Hollywood itself as the stars they carried about: showy, extravagant, transient, representing individual dreams and fantasies, ostentatious, exhibitionist, destined to be overtaken by time and superseded by later, more fashionable models. It was no coincidence that the ageing Isotta Fraschini in *Sunset Boulevard* represented passé, decadent Hollywood as much as the character of Norma Desmond. Neither was it by chance that Valentino was photographed at the wheel of his Voisin almost as much as he posed with Pola Negri.

With the demise of the star system it is the cars that have stayed. On one afternoon on Sunset Strip it is possible to see a constant parade of the most exotic and expensive cars – many of them costing as much as the average person thinks of spending on a house – in the world: Rolls-Royces, Mercedes, Ferraris, Lamborghinis, Maseratis, Aston-Martins, De Tomasos, Porsches proliferate among the Cadillacs, Lincolns, Buicks and Chryslers. And with the oil crisis many Americans have bought the economical European and Japanese automobiles as a saving for the two- and three-car family.

Amongst the millions of motor vehicles covering the surface of Chandlertown, there are still many dating from the days of Chandler's earliest short stories (1935 to the last – unfinished – novel in 1959) and cherished by their owners. They are common enough frequently to give a period look to a whole street or neighbourhood. Some of them are kept and paraded in *concours d'elegance* perfection; others are used as everyday transport, grimed with road dust, as rugged and dependable as when they first emerged from the showroom.

> I nosed around through the fog, didn't find anyone or see anyone, gave up bothering about that, and went along the blank side of the house to a curving line of palm trees and an old type arc light that hissed and flickered over the entrance to a sort of lane where I had stuck the 1925 Marmon touring car I still used for transportation. ('Finger Man')

That is one of Marlowe's first appearances in print and he has a nine-year-old car. Later, in the novels of the forties, his income still only runs to a small Oldsmobile coupé. Not that he failed to appreciate good quality machinery when he saw it, even if he had no particular personal longing for something exciting:

Los Angeles is the world's supreme example of the automotive society. Apart from a constant parade of expensive and custom-built cars, beautifully preserved examples of thirties and forties models are a commonplace feature of the streets

---

He drove me in a rust-coloured Jowett Jupiter with a flimsy canvas top under which there was only just room for the two of us. It had pale leather upholstery and what looked like silver fittings. I'm not too fussy about cars, but the damn thing did make my mouth water a little. He said it would do sixty-five in second. It had a squatty little gear shift that barely came up to my knee. (*The Long Goodbye*)

In fact, the Jowett Jupiter was not an exotic car. A small roadster with a good performance (it had several racing successes), it was hardly in the same class as, say, the Ferraris and Porsches which were beginning to be imported in the fifties. Still, a nice little toy to catch a rich man's (and Marlowe's) eye.

Whatever Marlowe may have said about not being fussy about cars, in the unfinished novel, *The Poodle Springs Story*, he enthuses over the car belonging to his recently acquired millionairess wife, Linda Loring.

> I pushed down on the accelerator. A cheap car would have stalled, but not the [Cadillac] Fleetwood. It smashed hard into the rear end of the [Buick] Roadmaster. I couldn't see what it did to the Fleetwood. There might be a small scratch or two on the front bumper.

But Marlowe uses the car as a symbol of his wedded independence.

> 'May I borrow the Fleetwood for a little while? Tomorrow I'll fly to LA and pick up my Olds.'
> 'Darling, does it have to be this way? It seems so unnecessary.'
> 'For me there isn't any other way,' I said. (*The Poodle Springs Story*)

Marlowe was determined not to be a kept man and a flashy car would be anathema to him – especially if it had not been bought with his own money. Not that a Cadillac Fleetwood would be so very ostentatious in Chandlertown. There is no need to comment further on that extraordinary circus of cars to be seen in the city – but Marlowe shall have the last word:

> I read somewhere that a dick should always have a plain, dark, inconspicuous car that nobody would notice. The guy had never been to LA. In LA to be conspicuous you would have to drive a flesh-pink Mercedes-Benz with a sun-porch on the roof and three pretty girls sun-bathing. (*Playback*)

11

I'LL TAKE THE BIG, SORDID, DIRTY CITY

Marlowe never seems to have been interested in what we might call the good things of life. Good morals rather than good meals were his basic criteria and if 'a man is what he eats' were true, then Marlowe was not much of a man.

In day-to-day life his demands were meagre: a small, dingy, dusty office, scrappy meals, shiny suits, a hat, a raincoat, a gun and a small car, he set no store by material things. It isn't that he failed to recognize quality when he saw it – clothes, cars, books, furniture, carpets, pictures (with reservations) are often observed and remarked upon for their craftsmanship and quality. But they were the accoutrements of the rich, and the rich in Marlowe's book were, as we know, almost all phoneys or worse; the luxuries with which they surrounded themselves were palpable evidence of their need to keep up a façade.

When the case on which Marlowe happened to be working (perhaps, also, the book on which Chandler happened to be working) was not going so well, he often mused to himself wearily, cynically, bitterly, but there are few instances of his own personal philosophy more directly expressed than this exchange with Menendez, the big-time racketeer of *The Long Goodbye*.

'I'm a big man, Marlowe. I make lots of dough. I got to make lots of dough to juice the guys I got to juice in order to make lots of dough to juice the guys I got to juice. I got a place in Bel Air that cost ninety grand and I already spent more than that to fix it up. I got a lovely platinum blonde wife and two kids in private schools back east. My wife's got an hundred and fifty grand in rocks and another seventy-five in furs and clothes. I got a butler, two maids, a cook, a chauffeur, not counting the monkey that walks behind me. Everywhere I go I'm a darling. The best of everything, the best food, the best drinks, the best clothes, the best hotel suites. I got a place in Florida and a seagoing yacht with a crew of five men. I got a Bentley, two Cadillacs, a Chrysler station wagon, and an MG for my boy. Couple of years my girl gets one too. What you got?'

'Not much,' I said. 'This year I have a house to live in – all to myself.'

'No woman?'

'Just me. In addition to that I have what you see here [Marlowe's office] and twelve hundred dollars in the bank and a few thousand in bonds. That answer your question?'

It may not answer the reader's question: why was Marlowe, who was well educated – 'a couple of years at college, either at the University of Oregon at Eugene, or Oregon State University at Corvallis, Oregon'* – satisfied with such a frugal existence? He occasionally went to the movies, occasionally listened to music (though we are not always told *what*), played chess with himself, never went to the theatre or concerts, although he accepted, if not appreciated, serious music. In *The Little Sister* Marlowe talks to a cop who plays the piano – 'Mozart and Bach mostly' – and contemplates him in a way that indicates some knowledge.

> You could see he was a man who loved to move his hands, to make neat inconspicuous motions with them, motions without any special meaning, but smooth and flowing and light as swansdown. They gave him a feel of delicate things delicately done, but not weak. Mozart, all right. I could see that.

Yes, Mozart was all right by Marlowe, but he was not so happy with modern composers:

> At 3 a.m. I was walking the floor and listening to Katchaturian working in a tractor factory. He called it a violin concerto. I called it a loose fan belt and the hell with it.

He was just as caustic about modern art:

> I lit a Camel, blew smoke through my nose and looked at a piece of black shiny metal on a stand. It showed a full, smooth curve with a shallow fold in it and two protuberances on the curve. I stared at it. Marriott saw me staring at it.
> 'An interesting bit,' he said negligently, 'I picked it up just the other day. Asta Dial's *Spirit of Dawn*.'
> 'I thought it was Klopstein's *Two Warts on a Fanny*,' I said. (*Farewell, My Lovely*)

Marlowe was always quick to put down any form of pretension.

His other comparatively long, self-analytical exposition on why he lived alone, simply, without anything which could remotely be called style, comes in *The Long Goodbye*, the most revelatory of the novels:

> The other part of me wanted to get out and stay out, but this was the part I never listened to. Because if I ever had I would have stayed in the town where I was born [Santa Rosa, about a hundred miles north of San Francisco] and worked in the hardware store and married the boss's daughter and had five

*Letter to Mr D.J. Ibberson, *Raymond Chandler Speaking*.

kids and read them the funny papers on Sunday morning and smacked their heads when they got out of line and squabbled with the wife about how much spending money they were to get and what programmes they could have on the radio or TV set. I might even have got rich – small-town rich, an eight-room house, two cars in the garage, chicken every Sunday and the *Reader's Digest* on the living-room table, the wife with a cast iron permanent and me with a brain like a sack of Portland cement. You take it, friend, I'll take the big, sordid, dirty city.

Well, yes! One can see that Marlowe would despise the smugness of middle-class life with the same intensity as the dropouts who left it for somewhat similar reasons in the sixties; but Chandlertown is not just 'a big, sordid, dirty city'. By comparison with London or New York its cultural delights are comparatively few: it is a city offering beaches and ball games and poolside barbecues rather than opera and ballet, but it *does*, and did *then*, have the Los Angeles Philharmonic Orchestra (not to be compared, admittedly, in Marlowe's day with its international standing now) and a handful of theatres, even if they were mostly showing revivals of past successes.

But why are we so anxious that Marlowe should have exercised his mind on the cultural delights of Chandlertown? After all, he was only a fictional private eye, not a real person, merely a character in some detective novels, however cleverly and entertainingly written. It is, of course, for that very reason, that they were such a reflection of the city, did so accurately record the modes and manners, mores and morals of the Angelinos, that one takes Marlowe as the chorus to Chandler's town, registering his views on the passing show as if he were some Olympian observer (Mount Olympus is a hill in Hollywood, newly developed for the newly rich) of his chosen milieu. There is some irony in the fact that Chandler's bleak thrillers are probably more illuminating about two or three decades of Los Angeles's history than any official documents.

Los Angeles has never been one of the world's cultural centres, despite the presence of a tremendous pool of talent attracted and employed by the movie industry. Composers like Schoenberg, writers like Isherwood, painters like Hockney have settled and worked there, but they were and are, by the nature of their profession, working in isolation. What is surprising is that the many distinguished and celebrated producers, directors, actors, singers and dancers who are more or less permanently resident in the city have never got together and created a repertory theatre, an opera or a ballet company of any renown, although companies from the East Coast or from overseas always receive enthusiastic welcomes and large, appreciative houses.

Another surprising comparative rarity is good restaurants. There is one outstanding one and two or three which have been famous – more for their clientele than for their cuisine – since the thirties but which are nowadays shamelessly trading on their reputations.

Marlowe was indifferent to good food, though frequently critical when it was bad. His only personal indulgences, it seems, were good coffee and good tobacco – and occasionally a bottle of good whisky, either rye or scotch. When he was out he would order a variety of drinks from a dry martini to a brandy, though never a fancy cocktail. Frequently a predinner drink would be followed by a rotten meal:

> I gobbled a dry martini and hurried back through the reed curtain to the dining room.
>
> The eighty-five cent dinner tasted like a discarded mail-bag and was served to me by a waiter who looked as if he would slug me for a quarter, cut my throat for six bits and bury me at sea in a barrel of concrete for a dollar and a half plus sales tax. (*Farewell, My Lovely*)

He was even more dismissive of those restaurants with pretensions:

> I closed for the day too, and drove over to La Cienaga to Rudy's Bar-B-Q, gave my name to the master of ceremonies and waited for the big moment on a bar stool with a whisky sour in front of me and Marek Weber's waltz music in my ears. After a while I got in past the velvet rope and ate one of Rudy's 'world-famous' Salisbury steaks which is hamburger on a slab of burnt wood, ringed with browned-over mashed potato, supported by fried onion rings and one of those mixed-up salads which men will eat with complete docility in restaurants, although they would probably start yelling if their wives tried to feed them one at home. (*The Long Goodbye*)

The fast-turnover restaurant with its conveyer belt system also received the Marlowe mark of disapproval – but he used it just the same:

> I ate dinner at a place near Thousand Oaks. Bad but quick. Feed 'em and throw 'em out. Lots of business. We can't bother with you sitting over your second cup of coffee, mister. You're using money space. See those people over there behind the rope? They want to eat. Anyway they think they have to. God knows why they want to eat here. They could do better out of a can. They're just restless. Like you. They have to get the car out and go somewhere. Sucker-bait for the racketeers that have taken over the restaurants.... I paid off and stopped in a bar to drop a brandy on top of the New York cut. (*The Little Sister*)

What could be more telling than that description of a city's eating habits – the citizens getting out their cars to drive down the endless highways to a fifth-rate restaurant? Except perhaps this:

> I went down to the drugstore and ate a chicken salad sandwich and drank some coffee. The coffee was overstrained and the sandwich was as full of rich

flavour as a piece torn off an old shirt. Americans will eat anything if it is toasted and held together with a couple of toothpicks and has lettuce sticking out of its sides, preferably a little wilted. (*The Long Goodbye*)

Sometimes even Marlowe could not stomach the idea of the quick-snack counters and hamburger drive-ins:

I drove on past the gaudy neons and the false fronts behind them, the sleazy hamburger joints that look like palaces under the colours, the circular drive-ins as gay as circuses with the chipper hard-eyed car-hops, the brilliant counters and the sweaty, greasy kitchens that would have poisoned a toad. (*The Little Sister*)

They did not poison Marlowe, however, when he bothered to stop.

Down at the drug-store lunch counter I had time to inhale two cups of coffee and a melted cheese sandwich with two slivers of ersatz bacon embedded in it, like dead fish in the silt at the bottom of a drained pool. (*The Little Sister*)

It is still very easy to find that sort of snack counter today, but to be fair it is as easy to find a clean, efficient, comfortable, welcoming restaurant/café/coffee house/hamburger-joint serving good meals at reasonable prices. In fact, it is entirely on the level of simple value-for-money meals – a hamburger made with real steak (not minced offal plus soya bean), crisp, fresh salad with a good dressing, roll and butter and as much coffee as you can drink for about £2 – at which the Americans excel and of which there is no European equivalent.

It is at so-called *haute cuisine* that the Chandlertown restaurants are generally bad. The more you pay the more pretentious and unsatisfactory the food. The menus are enormous, there is a great amount of flourish and flummery around the table, lots of obsequious bowing and scraping, and the main courses all come with the same frozen vegetables, the same mixed salads whether you want them or not. Understandably Marlowe did not care for that. In his day most of them – flashy restaurants-cum-nightclubs-cum-gambling casinos – were tied up with big-time crooks:

Now we get characters like this Steelgrave owning restaurants.... We've got the flash restaurants and nightclubs they run, and the hotels and apartment houses they own, and the grifters and con men and female bandits that live in them. The luxury trades, the pansy decorators, the Lesbian dress designers, the riff-raff of a big hard-boiled city with no more personality than a paper cup. (*The Little Sister*)

Obviously Marlowe hated such places – irrespective of whether they served good, bad or indifferent food, or provided good service – because of the racketeers who ran them. In Los Angeles I have visited restaurants and nightclubs reputedly run by the Mafia which is still generally accepted as the major entrepreneur operating some of the city's most elegant enterprises.

Marlowe was frequently disdainful not only of the restaurants and nightclubs and hotels and apartment houses, but of the city itself; he felt that as it grew its character faded – and what character it did possess emanated from Hollywood:

> Real cities have something else, some individual bony structure under the muck. Los Angeles has Hollywood – and hates it. It ought to consider itself damn lucky. Without Hollywood it would be a mail-order city. Everything in the catalogue you could get better somewhere else. (*The Little Sister*)

True – up to a point. Hollywood has always given Los Angeles much of its character, both good and bad, but there were other localities, suburbs that were once small villages and communities, each with its own distinct style and ambience, which have now been welded into the vast metropolis. Marlowe saw it happening and regretted the submersion of distinct characteristics into overall similarities, a regret that was at odds with his proclaimed rejection of anything that could give quality to his mode of existence:

> 'I used to like this town,' I said, just to be saying something and not to be thinking too hard. 'A long time ago. There were trees along Wilshire Boulevard. Beverly Hills was a country town. Westwood was bare hills and lots offering at eleven hundred dollars and no takers. Hollywood was a bunch of frame houses on the inter-urban line. Los Angeles was just a big, dry sunny place with ugly homes and no style, but good hearted and peaceful. It had the climate they just yap about now. People used to sleep out on porches. Little groups who thought they were intellectual used to call it the Athens of America. It wasn't that, but it wasn't a neon lighted slum, either.' (*The Little Sister*)

Chandler speaking, or Marlowe? It does not reflect modern Los Angeles very accurately.

Wilshire Boulevard still has trees planted down part of its length – that part which goes through exclusive Beverly Hills, which is both an elegant shopping area and a residential district of magnificent homes. Westwood was given commercial impetus in the mid-1920s with the establishment of a Chamber of Commerce. No chance of obtaining 'lots offering at eleven hundred dollars' today, or even at a hundred times that amount. Parts of early Westwood village are still visible – the first bank established there, some period cinemas, some old apartment blocks – but now they are overshadowed by huge commercial buildings.

Marlowe was equally caustic about the generally jerry-built quality of Chandlertown houses:

> About the only part of a California house you can't put your foot through is the front door. (*The Big Sleep*)

An exaggeration founded on truth. In such a perennially warm climate it is not so necessary to build in a way that is going to keep out icy draughts. In Bel Air, I have visited beautiful and expensive homes where it was possible to observe daylight between the walls and the windowframe; many of Los Angeles's houses and apartment buildings are still built on the wood-frame plaster-covered principle. And it is common to refer to a house which has been standing for twenty years as 'old'.

While much of Chandlertown survives the ravages of time, other parts succumb to what is known as a 'transhent [transient] city', built only to last a decade or two. Some houses are even moved like prefabs, from one area to another as they became respectively run down or developed.

> Taggart Wilde, the District Attorney, lived at the corner of Fourth and Lafayette Park, in a white frame house the size of a carbarn, with red sandstone porte-cochere built on to one side and a couple of acres of soft rolling lawn in front. It was one of those solid old fashioned houses which it used to be the thing to move bodily to new locations as the city grew westward. (*The Big Sleep*)

There are still some old-fashioned houses in the residential streets around Lafayette Park, but the park and the immediate locality are now dominated by a huge new office building faced with pale blue mirror glass in which the local church, the park and houses are reflected.

Farther downtown lies the once exclusive Bunker Hill:

> Bunker Hill is old town, lost town, shabby town, crook town. Once, very long ago, it was the choice residential district of the city, and there are still standing a few of the jigsaw Gothic mansions with wide porches and walls covered with round-end shingles and full corner bay-windows with spindle turrets. They are all rooming houses now, their parquet floors are scratched and worn through the once glossy finish and the wide sweeping staircases are dark with time and with cheap varnish laid over generations of dirt. In the tall rooms hagged landladies bicker with shifty tenants. (*The High Window*)

Even the musicians have gone now; today Bunker Hill is surrounded by city skyscrapers, with razed building lots awaiting the developers. Only one or two decrepit apartment houses and hotels hang on, remnants of the 'shabby town, crook town' that Marlowe knew.

In The Big Sleep *'Taggart Wilde, the District Attorney, lived at the corner of Fourth and Lafayette Park.' In fact, typical of Chandler's deliberate misplacement, it is not Fourth but Sixth Street that is in conjunction with Lafayette Park. Even so, the area still contains many large houses like the one illustrated here and similar to the one in which Chandler's DA resided*

Perhaps this sense of endless shifting and changing, this rapid decay within a decade or two, is one of the reasons why Marlowe placed so little value on, cared so little for, the qualities of life in Chandlertown. Because of the very nature of his work, he might suddenly be cut off from it all. With no dependants, few friends, his handful of personal belongings and his rented apartment would hardly be a burden on whoever had to act as his executor. But his imperviousness to the good things of life stem from something deeper than that. Marlowe, like his creator, was, beneath the cynical exterior, a sensitive if not a sentimental man. Quality, for the average person, was something that no longer existed in the planned-obsolescence economy:

> 'In our time we have seen a shocking decline in both public and private morals. You can't expect *quality* [my italics] from people whose lives are subjected to a lack of quality. You can't have quality with mass production. You don't want it because it lasts too long. So you substitute styling, which is a commercial swindle intended to produce artificial obsolescence. Mass production couldn't sell its goods next year unless it made what it sold this year look unfashionable in a year from now. We have the whitest kitchens and the most shining bathrooms in the world. But in the lovely white kitchen the average American housewife can't produce a meal fit to eat, and the lovely shining bathroom is mostly a receptacle for deodorants, laxatives, sleeping pills and the products of that confidence racket called the cosmetic industry. We make the finest packages in the world, Mr Marlowe. The stuff inside is mostly junk.' (*The Long Goodbye*)

It is Chandler's cynical irony that this comprehensive condemnation of the American way of life is delivered to Marlowe by Harlan Potter, the multi-millionaire who was trying to hush up a murder, a man who could buy everything he wanted except Marlowe, even though, in the two chapters of the final, unfinished *The Poodle Springs Story*, Potter gets Marlowe as a son-in-law! Marlowe preferred to take the 'big, sordid, dirty city', with its transient trash, in preference to people like Harlan Potter who were the real blight in Chandlertown.

12
AN AGONIZING EXPERIENCE

The use that Chandler made of the Los Angeles area, the constant shifting of the action from Marlowe's office or apartment to various suburbs of the city, the perpetual movement, made the stories ideal for film adaptation. As well as this frequent change of scene, the interplay of interiors and exteriors, the 'open' structure of the stories, Chandler created sharply delineated characters and gave them equally sharp, terse, witty dialogue: all the ingredients for Hollywood melodrama – or, to coin a phrase for that particular genre of detective thriller, 'murder-drama'.

Curiously, however, Chandler made comparatively little use of the film industry itself – curiously, because the cinematic scene, long before Chandler began writing, was a hotbed of intrigue, scandal, vice and corruption; it even had its own quota of violent deaths. Perhaps the theme was too easy, too obvious; perhaps for a writer who would seem to be also a natural screenwriter, he felt the subject to be too incestuous, too provocative. And yet Chandler was quite prepared to publish his less than flattering views on the film factories and the men who ran them:

> To me the interesting point about Hollywood writers of talent is not how few or how many there are, but how little of worth their talent is allowed to achieve. Interesting – but hardly unexpected, once you accept the premise that writers are employed to write screenplays on the theory that, being writers, they have a particular gift and training for the job, and are then prevented from doing it with any independence or finality whatsoever, on the theory that, being merely writers, they know nothing about making pictures; and of course if they don't know how to make pictures, they couldn't possibly know how to write them. It takes a producer to tell them that.*

Chandler's acute, accurate, acerbic assessment (most of Hollywood thought of it as an attack) of 'the Hollywood system' holds true today,

*Article first published *Atlantic Monthly*, 1945; reprinted in *Raymond Chandler Speaking*.

years after the decline of the great studios and their partial resurrection. The generally dismissive attitude of stars, producers, directors and the typically faceless men of the front office towards the writer of any film project still exists.

Before he made use of the star/studio scene as part of the plot for *The Little Sister* (1948) Chandler had been involved with eight screenplays, four adapted from his own novels, the others either original screenplays or adaptations from the work of other writers. Before the reader reaches the sound stage, or the on-set squabbling, or Marlowe's interview with the rising star, Mavis Weld, which is the purpose of his visit, Chandler introduces the studio boss. He is a rather pathetic, lonely man, reduced to watching his prize boxer dogs urinate as a relaxation from the pressures of his job:

> The man whose name was not Wilson said lovingly: 'Always do it in the same order. Fascinates me.'
>
> 'Do what?' I asked.
>
> 'Pee,' he said. 'Question of seniority it seems. Very orderly. First Maisie. She's the mother. Then Mac. Year older than Jock, the baby. Always the same. Even in my office.'
>
> 'In your office?' I said, and nobody ever looked stupider saying anything.
>
> He lifted his whitish eyebrows at me, took a plain brown cigar out of his mouth, bit the end off and spat it in the pool. 'That won't do the fish any good,' I said.
>
> He gave me an up-from-under look. 'I raise boxers. The hell with fish.'
>
> I figured it was just Hollywood. I lit a cigarette and sat down on the bench. 'In your office,' I said. 'Well, every day has its new idea, hasn't it?'
>
> 'Up against the corner of the desk. Do it all the time. Drives my secretaries crazy. Gets into the carpet they say. What's the matter with women nowadays? Never bothers me. Rather like it. You get fond of dogs, you even like to watch them pee.'

That rather bizarre scene is entirely expendable. It tells us nothing about Marlowe or his current problem and is irrelevant to the plot. But it was Chandler having a little fun at the expense of Hollywood. Quite clearly the three dogs (Chandler was a fanatical cat-lover) urinating in strict order represent the rigid hierarchy of the studio executives, so rabidly conscious of their status and prestige. Yet Chandler, for all his cogent criticisms, was not bitter: he accepted the situation, was glad of the comparatively easy money and practised his craft with an undiminished professionalism within a system whose faults he observed with crystal clarity.

He knew, as so many other writers have done, that there was a great novel to be written about Hollywood.

I wish I could write the Hollywood novel that has never been written, but it takes a more photographic memory than I have. The whole scene is so complex and all of it would have to be in, or the thing would be just another distortion.*

Later on, in the same chapter of *The Little Sister*, Chandler obviously enjoys the sort of bitchy scene that he had doubtless witnessed himself while working on various pictures:

'Weld's timing is just right,' Gamman said. 'Her performance is just right, too.'

Susan Crawley shrugged elegantly. 'I had the impression she could speed it up a trifle, Ned. It's good, but it *could* be better.'

'If it was any better, darling,' Mavis Weld told her smoothly, 'somebody might call it acting. You wouldn't want anything like that to happen in *your* picture, would you?'

Torrence laughed. Susan Crawley turned and glared at him. 'What's funny, Mister Thirteen?'

Torrance's face settled into an icy mask. 'That name again?' he almost hissed.

'Good heavens, you mean you didn't know,' Susan Crawley said wonderingly. 'They all call you Mister Thirteen because any time you play a part it means twelve other guys have turned it down'.

That is another expendable scene but, again, Chandler was amusing himself. He had little time for the studio egos which consistently overshadowed the hapless writer and his craft.

The book, like the screenplays, was written at a time when the cinema was still the great popular culture, when the private and professional lives of the stars filled the gossip columns, provided the material for film magazines, influenced fashion and maintained a multitude of satellite industries and businesses. Television hastened the decline and collapse of many of the Hollywood studios, some of which are now enjoying a certain renaissance, although the film and television stars of Hollywood today are probably outnumbered, if not outranked, by the celebrities of the world pop-music scene.

It is a moot point whether Chandler's original screenplays, and those he created from the stories of other writers, were better than those he adapted from his own work. A novel is under the control of its creator; a film – as Chandler frequently deplored – is at the mercy of so many collaborators, several of whom have no aesthetic function but nevertheless influence the artistic integrity of the work.

In 1944 Chandler's first screenplay (for Paramount) with the director,

*Letter to Edward Weeks, in *Raymond Chandler Speaking*.

Billy Wilder, was an adaptation of James M. Cain's excellent novel, *Double Indemnity*. It was an excellent film, too, and Chandler was lucky in working on such fine basic material, with a good director and stars – Fred MacMurray, Barbara Stanwyck, Edward G. Robinson. Six years later, in a letter to Hamish Hamilton* he says:

> Working with Billy Wilder on *Double Indemnity* was an agonizing experience and has probably shortened my life, but I learned from it about as much about screen-writing as I am capable of learning, which is not very much.

Chandler was being modest; there is no doubt that he rapidly became an outstanding screenwriter with a sharp, instinctive understanding of its special requirements.

Chandler's next screenwriting chore (also for Paramount) was a curious one: adapting, with Frank Partos, Rachel Field's soap-opera novel *And Now Tomorrow* about a deaf socialite (Loretta Young) in love with her harsh doctor (Alan Ladd). A less likely subject for Raymond Chandler is hard to imagine. In the same year he collaborated with Hagar Wilde on the screenplay of *The Unseen*, a murder story directed by Lewis Allen; and then his own novel, *Farewell, My Lovely*, was used as the basis of the RKO film *Murder My Sweet*, of which the most notable element was Dick Powell playing his first tough-guy role. Many people thought him miscast as Marlowe.

In 1946 Chandler wrote an original screenplay, *The Blue Dahlia*, directed by George Marshall for Paramount, in which Alan Ladd and Veronica Lake acted as a successful team. Chandler, however, was very dissatisfied with the way in which the director interfered with the screenplay, so much so that he threatened to walk out:

> Also, what happens on the set is beyond the writer's control. In this case I threatened to walk off the picture, not yet finished, unless they stopped the director putting in fresh dialogue out of his head. As to the scenes of violence, I did not write them that way at all....†

It is a situation familiar to all writers who have written screenplays and suffered from producers and directors who think they know what is best.

In the same year as Chandler wrote *The Blue Dahlia* for Paramount, Warner's produced a film version of his novel *The Big Sleep* which was a minor masterpiece of its type. With perfect casting – Humphrey Bogart and Lauren Bacall – and splendid direction by Howard Hawks, who also acted as producer, the film is by far the best cinematic realization

---

*In *Raymond Chandler Speaking*.
†Letter to James Sandoe, in *Raymond Chandler Speaking*.

of a Chandler story. If Bogart's stature was a little small for Marlowe, his personality was very close to Chandler's psychological conception of the character: tough, laconic, wise-cracking, with a sense of moral integrity beneath the hard-bitten exterior. Bacall was equally well cast as the rich, sophisticated Mrs Regan, and both stars had the right chemistry to make a legendary acting team. Hawks – a very experienced director who had already directed Bogart and Bacall in their first film together, *To Have and Have Not* – brilliantly captured the atmosphere of decadence and menace in his treatment of the material. Chandler himself recognized it as an excellent film:

> When and if you see the film of *The Big Sleep* (the first half of it anyhow) you will realize what can be done with this sort of story by a director with the gift of atmosphere and the requisite touch of hidden sadism. Bogart, of course, is also so much better than any other tough-guy actor. As we say here, Bogart can be tough without a gun. Also he has a sense of humour that contains that grating undertone of contempt. Ladd is hard, bitter and occasionally charming, but he is after all a small boy's idea of a tough guy. Bogart is the genuine article. Like Edward G. Robinson, all he has to do to dominate a scene is to enter it.*

A year later (1947) two other Chandler stories were filmed: *The High Window* (*The Brasher Doubloon*) by 20th Century Fox, and *The Lady in the Lake* by MGM. Neither was particularly successful but *The Lady in the Lake*, which was directed by Robert Montgomery (who also 'starred' as the voice of Marlowe), used the 'subjective camera' technique about which Chandler was dismissive:

> The camera eye technique of *Lady in the Lake* is old stuff in Hollywood. Every young writer or director has wanted to try it. 'Let's make the camera a character'; it's been said at every lunch table in Hollywood one time or another.†

Chandler was bored doing the screenplay, too:

> I am working on a screen treatment of *The Lady in the Lake*.... The last time I'll ever do a screenplay of a book I wrote myself. Just turning over dry bones.‡

In 1950 Chandler was engaged on adapting a novel by Patricia Highsmith, *Strangers on a Train*, for the screen. Doubtless he was pleased to do it because it was to be directed by Alfred Hitchcock, but he was dubious about the story as he thought that it was based on an absurd premise and felt that it would be difficult to suspend the audience's disbelief:

*Letter to Hamish Hamilton, in *Raymond Chandler Speaking*.
†Letter to Alex Barris, in *Raymond Chandler Speaking*.
‡Letter to James Sandoe, in *Raymond Chandler Speaking*.

I nearly went crazy myself trying to block out this scene. I hate to say how many times I did it. It's darn near impossible to write, because consider what you have to put over:

(1) A perfectly decent young man agrees to murder a man he doesn't know, has never seen, in order to keep a maniac from giving himself away and from tormenting the nice young man.

(2) From a character point of view, the audience will not believe the nice young man is going to kill anybody, or has any idea of killing anybody.*

Chandler also had reservations about Hitchcock's directorial approach, although he liked Hitch himself:

The thing that amuses me about Hitchcock is the way he directs a film in his head before he knows what the story is. You find yourself trying to rationalize the shots he wants to make rather than the story. Every time you get set he jabs you off balance by wanting to do a love scene on top of the Jefferson Memorial or something like that. He has a strong feeling for stage business and mood and background, not so much for the guts of the business, I guess that's why some of his pictures lose their grip on logic and turn into wild chases.†

Chandler's criticism is very perceptive: Hitchcock *is* often concerned with setpieces rather than with the logical development of plot and character. Nevertheless, *Strangers on a Train* was one of Hitchcock's best works, helped considerably by Chandler's script (with Czenzi Ormonde) which wholly succeeded in suspending disbelief.

Chandler's last novel, *Playback*, was first written as a screenplay for Universal-International, who never produced it. It is, perhaps, his least satisfactory work and reflects what he himself called his 'tired mind' and the alcoholic depression and loneliness he was enduring after the death of his wife. On the other hand, *The Long Goodbye*, which I consider in many ways to be his best novel, was written during the almost equally dispiriting period of Cissy's final illness. Chandler himself considered *Farewell, My Lovely* to be the best of his works and *The High Window* the worst. But that opinion was expressed in 1949, before *The Little Sister*, *The Long Goodbye* and *Playback* had been written.

After Chandler died, *The Little Sister* was made into a film by MGM under the title *Marlowe*. It was directed by Paul Bogart and was eminently forgettable. Chandler would not have been amused.

More recently there have been two more Marlowe movies: an original adaptation of *The Long Goodbye* directed by Robert Altman, and a

*From 'Notes about the Screenplay', in *Raymond Chandler Speaking*.
†From a letter to Hamish Hamilton, in *Raymond Chandler Speaking*.

careful second remake of *Farewell, My Lovely*. (The first version, made by RKO in 1942, was called *The Falcon Takes Over*.)

Altman's film is set in contemporary Los Angeles. While much of the city and the life style of its inhabitants is unchanged from Chandler's day, there are several elements that are new – additional rather than different. For instance, the emphasis on youth and the general permissiveness of modern Chandlertown.

In Chandler's time the moral laxity was there, especially for those who could pay for it; the great change that has taken place in the last twenty years is the *general* immorality, the ease with which every form of decadent pleasure can be satisfied, the prevalence of gambling, drug-taking, sexual promiscuity. Altman has used this to considerable effect, just as he has preserved that other hallmark of a Marlowe story, its mobility, moving from Marlowe's scruffy apartment in Hollywood to his client's opulent beach house at Malibu, from the trendy office of the racketeer to the noisy, downtown police precinct. The plot has been simplified to the point of emasculation, but what Chandler would certainly not recognize is the character of Philip Marlowe. Played by Elliot Gould, he is shambling, unshaven, unkempt, living in real squalor. Chandler's Marlowe may have had a dusty office, but he always tidied up his own apartment and his personal fastidiousness was irreproachable – he was frequently showering and changing his linen. Most important of all, the Marlowe of the novels would never, *never* have committed a premeditated, cold-blooded murder. While Altman's film was technically brilliant, beautifully photographed and acted and, in its own way, reflected the multifaceted fascination of the Los Angeles location, the character of Marlowe as conceived by Chandler was in no way discernible in the writing, playing or direction.

A different approach altogether is the second remake of *Farewell, My Lovely*. Directed by Dick Richards, with Robert Mitchum as Marlowe and Charlotte Rampling as the murderous Mrs Grayle, the film possesses a self-conscious artistry that was not present in the previous versions. It is a deliberate piece of Hollywood pastiche, not only in its use of architecture and interior design, cars and artifacts, but in its carefully calculated creation of mood through lighting and soundtrack. (In the earlier versions the most perfunctory set dressings were used, everything was patently 'studio', with no attempt to recreate what were then the current modes.) Although its use of colour, exterior locations and more overt sex and sadism places it at one remove – to be precise, some thirty-five years – from the original, it was produced with absolute faithfulness to the style and manner not only of Chandler's novels, but also the films that were made of them in the forties.

Although he came to the role some years or so too late, Mitchum is arguably the perfect casting for Marlowe. His height, his naturally weary, cynical expression, his tough-guy presence, his laconic delivery make him the exact physical realization of the character from the printed page. He is just ten or twelve years older than Chandler's estimate of Marlowe's age. Charlotte Rampling, too, is an excellent substitute for Lauren Bacall (who was not, of course, either in the original or the first remake, but is the epitome of those forties *femmes fatales*). Rampling displays a dangerously seductive quality, the ability to suggest something menacing beneath the veneer of sexy sophistication. As the forlorn, massive Moose Malloy, Jack O'Halloran is an acceptable replacement for Mike Mazurki who gave a notable performance in *Murder My Sweet*.

More important than either the directing or the casting, however, is the art direction of Dean Tavoularis, who meticulously recreated the interiors of the period.

The film, in fact, demonstrates the point that I have reiterated throughout this book: the considerable remains of genuine old Chandlertown that survive into the seventies are not difficult to find. Very little was needed to dress the exteriors, apart from minor changes to street furniture – lamps, seats, signs – and major period sets – the Grayle mansion, the Menendez nightclub-casino, Florian's dine-and-dice emporium, Jessie Florian's delapidated frame bungalow, Marlowe's office block, and the cars – were all there waiting to be utilized with the minimum of alteration, redecoration or redesign. Only the long-gone gambling ship had to be built.

It is interesting to compare the remake of *Farewell, My Lovely* with, for example, *The Big Sleep*. In that film the comparatively few exterior shots were all done in the studio. The Sternwood mansion, Geiger's bookstore on Hollywood Boulevard, his house in Laurel Canyon were all constructed on the Warner back lot. Paradoxically, the *Farewell, My Lovely* remake – giving reality to the fiction – is more authentic in its use of actual exteriors, a haunting piece of time travel back to forties Chandlertown.

13

THE CHIMPANZEE WHO PLAYED THE VIOLIN

The television series of Chandler's short stories, produced by David Wicks Television for LWT as 'Marlowe: Private Eye' encapsulates almost all of Chandler's fiction. They not only encompass the full span of his writing career, from 'Blackmailers Don't Shoot' (1933) to 'The Pencil' (1959 – originally published under the title 'Marlowe Takes on the Syndicate'), but chart the development of Marlowe himself and, almost as important, utilize the Los Angeles environment with graphic precision.

Yet Chandler was dismissive of television. In 1950 he wrote to his agent:

> I've spent a little time lately looking at television for the first time and my opinion is that the people who look at television for any length of time and with any regularity have not ceased to read. They never began. It's a great deal like the chimpanzee who played the violin. He didn't play it in tune; he didn't play anything recognizable as a melody; he didn't hold the bow right; he didn't finger correctly. But, Jesus, wasn't it wonderful that he could play the violin at all.

Which, of course, is a rather clumsy crib on Samuel Johnson's remark about a woman preaching: '... like a dog's walking on his hinder legs. It is not done well; but you are surprised to find it done at all.' Chandler went on:

> The writing, I suppose, is no worse than it was in lots of radio shows, but by being more intrusive it seems worse. If you have spent fifteen years building up a character you can't deliver him to the sort of people that do these shows. I don't think the plots are terribly important. But I think the actor and the dialogue are very important – so much so that if I were offered a television show (which I have not been) I would have to demand approval of the actor playing Philip Marlowe and also script approval. I simply can't afford to have this character murdered by a bunch of yucks.

Despite his antipathy to television Chandler acquiesced in the transmission of a version of *The Little Sister* and agreed to let CBS make a pilot film, which was never sold, of a series to be based on Marlowe, just as there had been a successful NBC radio series of Marlowe adventures written by a number of other writers. So it is permissible, on the basis of that revealing remark '... if I were offered a television show ...', to speculate about how and what he would have written for the medium had he been asked. For, although he complained about the way Hollywood treated writers, there is no doubt he obtained a certain amount of satisfaction from knowing that his scripts were regarded as models of their type, that films like *The Big Sleep* and *Double Indemnity* were, even in their own day, classics of the genre. And the ability to set similar standards for television would surely have been an incentive, quite apart from the money.

But television was then very much in its infancy and no one, it seems, made a sufficiently attractive offer to lure Chandler into being a pioneer. It is not surprising, therefore, that he makes only the briefest reference to the medium in *The Long Goodbye* (when Marlowe is musing about what it would have been like to be an ordinary family man) without, as one might have expected, any passing aside about the immense power for good or evil that television possesses. Another decade and he might have rectified that – and even, perhaps, have written one of his surgically analytical essays on the subject. That is our loss.

Our limited gain has been that it wasn't long before Chandler's conception of the private eye as a popular folk hero found its way on to our small screens – with the qualification that some variations on Chandler's prototype have been good and others not. His own proto-types for Marlowe appear in the short stories under such aliases as Steve Grace, Johnny Dalmas and, simply, Mallory, in 'Blackmailers Don't Shoot':

> The man in the powder-blue suit – which wasn't powder blue under the lights of the Club Bolivar – was tall, with wide-set grey eyes, a thin nose, a jaw of stone. He had a rather sensitive mouth. His hair was crisp and black, ever so faintly touched with grey, as by an almost diffident hand. His clothes fitted him as though they had a soul of their own, not just a doubtful past. His name happened to be Mallory.

The powder-blue suit sounds a little doubtful, but the rest of the description would serve for Marlowe in any of Chandler's subsequent stories. In fact this first story carries within its pages many of the seeds which sprouted within Chandler's later *oeuvre*. There is Landrey, would-be Hollywood actor turned racketeer, who dies by the gun when his way of life turns sour. There is Mardonne, his partner in a gambling club, characterized by 'a soft, husky voice, the voice of a fat man, but he was not fat'. His trigger-happy bodyguard is obviously homosexual, a forerunner of the leather-jacketed lover/strong-arm guy Carel Lundgren in *The Big Sleep*:

> The blond young man got off the desk, yawned, put his hand to his mouth with an affected flirt of the wrist. There was a large diamond on one of his fingers. He looked at Mallory, smiled, and went slowly out of the room, closing the door.

Later, when he returns, gun in hand, Mallory refers to him as 'the gay caballero', an amusing Chandlerism in which he unconsciously anticipated today's vernacular for the homosexual.

Within the story there is also a corrupt cop, with all the nasty habits – drunkenness, sadism – of the corrupt cops in later stories; there is Erno, a small, dark Latin type, also handy with a gun, forerunner of a number of Mexicans, Italians and Filipinos ('spigs', 'wops' and 'flips', as Chandler's characters contemptuously refer to them) always on the fringe of the criminal class in later stories; Costello, another racketeer with unpleasant physical characteristics: 'a ludicrous, big bulbous nose, no eyebrows at all, hair the colour of the inside of a sardine can'. And there is Cathcart, one of a subsequent number of big, tough, weary, police chiefs going to seed:

> Cathcart was a big, shabby Irishman with a sweaty face and a loose-lipped grin. His white moustache was stained in the middle with nicotine. His hands had a lot of warts on them.

An even more physically unpleasant specimen than the crooks!

The women, too, prefigure most of Chandler's predatory females. There is Rhonda Farr, tough-talking Hollywood star, subject to blackmail:

> Rhonda Farr was very beautiful. She was wearing, for this occasion, all black, except a collar of white fur, light as thistledown, on her evening wrap. Except also a white wig which, meant to disguise her [it goes without saying that under the wig she is blonde], made her look very girlish. Her eyes were cornflower blue and she had the sort of skin an old rake dreams of.

Despite the veneer of toughness Mallory is allowed a grudging admiration for her courage. And later, when he returns with the indiscreet love letters for which she was being blackmailed, and she greets him in 'jade-green lounging pyjamas', their hard-boiled dialogue ends in a kiss:

> Mallory reached out and picked up his hat. 'You're a hell of a guy,' he said, grinning. 'Christ! but you Hollywood frails must be hard to get on with!'
> He leaned forward suddenly, put his left hand behind her head and kissed her on the mouth hard. Then he flipped the tips of his fingers across her cheek.

Perfect Marlowe stuff, exactly like his behaviour with Mavis Weld in *The Little Sister*, with the murderous Mrs Grayle in *Farewell, My Lovely*, with Linda Loring in *The Long Goodbye*, with Mrs Regan in *The Big Sleep*.

The secondary female character in 'Blackmailers Don't Shoot' – and it is a very brief, but telling, appearance – is not even named, just called 'the thin woman':

> An unshaded light bulb hung from the middle of the ceiling. A thin woman in a dirty white smock stood under it, limp arms at her sides. Dull, colourless eyes brooded under a mop of rusty hair. Her fingers fluttered and twitched in involuntary contraction of the muscles. She made a thin plaintive sound, like a starved cat. [Later] The woman in the smock wetted her lips. 'A shot of M,' she said in a slack voice. 'No harm done, Mister.'

This dismal creature has been in charge of the kidnapped Rhonda Farr, the wife of a dope peddler, and she is typical of the female losers manipulated by the big-time racketeers, forerunner of the sad Agnes Lozelle in *The Big Sleep*. Like her, the 'thin woman' is allowed to make her getaway when all the big crooks are accounted for at the end of the story.

Subsequent short stories develop Chandler's twin symbols of evil, corrupt officialdom and venal big business, later to come to fruition in *The Big Sleep* and *Farewell, My Lovely*. Here is the revealing description of Frank Dorr, 'the big politico you have to see if you want to open a gambling hell or a bawdy house' in 'Finger Man' (1934):

> He was the kind of man who loved to have a desk in front of him, and shove his fat stomach against it, and fiddle with things on it, and look very wise. He had a fat, muddy face, a thin fringe of white hair stuck up a little, small sharp eyes, small and very delicate hands.

The fatness, the small eyes and the delicate hands are all physical features that Chandler reserved for his more odious male characters, a gift to any film or television casting director.

In the same story there is Canales – a Latin, of course – the oily operator of a crooked gambling establishment:

> A door opened at the end of the tables and a very slight, very pale man came into the room. He had straight, lustreless black hair, a high, bony forehead, flat, impenetrable eyes. He had a thin moustache that was trimmed in two sharp lines almost at right-angles to each other. They came down below the corner of his mouth a full inch. The effect was Oriental. His skin had a thick, glistening pallor.
>
> He slid behind the croupière, stopped at a corner of the centre table, glanced at the red-haired girl and touched the ends of his moustache with two fingers, the nails of which had a purplish tint.

Nearly all of Chandler's villains have small or fat or delicate hands with exquisitely manicured nails! In the final, very bloody shoot-out, Canales shoots Dorr through the eye and is himself gunned down by one of Dorr's henchmen in his dying moments. The story ends with another cynical hint at corruption:

> Miss Glenn made a clean getaway [another female loser allowed to escape police retribution] and was never heard of again. I think that's about all, except that I had to turn the twenty-two grand over to the Public Administrator. He allowed me two hundred dollars fee and nine dollars and twenty cents mileage. Sometimes I wonder what he did with the rest of it.

Yet, with this gallery of archetypal figures, it is Marlowe who remains the king pin, the hinge, the pivot upon which the plot turns, and it is interesting to note that in all the novels Chandler uses the first person singular, as he does in four of the fourteen short stories. Whether he appears as Mallory, or Steve Grayce or Johnny Dalmas (he is called Marlowe, of course, in the television series), he has all of Marlowe's characteristics: he is tough, world-weary, cynical, something of a misogynist – yet susceptible to women. In the last story, 'The Pencil', he has developed one part of his personality that simply isn't there until *The Long Goodbye* (1954): the yearning for the comforting routine, the stability of marriage. Chandler spells it out in the last story he wrote ('the first Marlowe short story in twenty years and written specially for England'). Here is the exchange between Marlowe and Anne Riordan at the beginning of the story:

> 'You're the damndest guy,' she said. 'Women do anything you want them to. How come I'm still a virgin at twenty-eight?'
> 'We need a few like you. Why don't you get married?'
> 'To what? Some cynical chaser who has nothing left but technique? I don't know any really nice men – except you. I'm no pushover for white teeth and a gaudy smile.'
> I went over and pulled her to her feet. I kissed her long and hard. 'I'm honest,' I almost whispered. 'That's something. But I'm too shop-soiled for a girl like you. I've thought of you, I've wanted you but that sweet clear look in your eyes tells me to lay off.'
> 'Take me,' she said softly. 'I have dreams too.'
> 'I couldn't. It's not the first time it's happened to me. I've had too many women to deserve one like you. We have to save a man's life. I'm going.'
> She stood up and watched me leave with a grave face.
> The women you get and the women you don't get – they live in different worlds. I don't sneer at either world. I live in both myself.

That dialogue neatly encapsulates the difference between Mallory and Marlowe, but it is really more of a development than a difference. 'The Pencil' comes closest to our own times with its references to the beatnik generation and Los Angeles International Airport and its theme of a new type of Mafia, not the street warfare, gang-killers of the Prohibition era who had fed Chandler's early material, but the low-profile, sober-suited, executive-type hit men of today. All the other stories in the television series belong to the thirties and the producer has, quite rightly, placed them all in that period, carefully recreating the clothes, the cars, the artifacts, the music of the time.

Yet for all the fastidious attention to period detail, the stories emerge as splendid, fast-moving thriller material, not just as empty exercises in style. And it is Chandler's constant use of the vast Los Angeles conurbation in the stories that provides a fascinating setting for Marlowe's adventures. During the time it has taken to research and assemble the material for this book, the Los Angeles authorities have

Los Feliz is a long, beautiful boulevard lined with many Spanish-Colonial-style houses built in the twenties and thirties when the style was very popular. Chandler often makes use of this area, beginning with the early short story 'Nevada Gas', one of the 'Philip Marlowe, Private Eye' series

begun to realize just what architectural and environmental gems they possess and have accordingly made moves to reclaim, maintain and preserve them. Much, of course, has been irretrievably lost, particularly in the downtown area of the City of Los Angeles itself, the location of City Hall and the area of Bunker Hill, so sharply described in 'The King in Yellow':

> Court Street was old town, wop town, crook town, arty town. It lay across the top of Bunker Hill and you could find anything there from down-at-heels ex-Greenwich-Villagers to crooks on the lam, from ladies of anybody's evening to County Relief clients brawling with haggard landladies in grand old houses with scrolled porches, parquetry floors, and immense sweeping banisters of white oak, mahogany and Circassian walnut. It had been a nice place once, had Bunker Hill, and from the days of its niceness there still remained the funny little funicular railway, called Angel's Flight, which crawled up and down a yellow clay bank from Hill Street.

It is worth comparing this description with the one of the same area in *The High Window*.* The grand old houses have all disappeared from the area now, making way for the towering new skyscrapers, the Dorothy Chandler (no relation!) arts complex and glittering hotels. Yet the little funicular railway is reportedly to be restored. Not far away, however, and still downtown in what is now predominantly a Mexican area, there still remain some grand old houses, while bang in the city itself, there are one or two magnificent old cinemas with Art-Deco façades and interiors, catering almost entirely for the Spanish-speaking residents. And not half a dozen blocks away the television producers found two ideal locations for filming, West Washington Boulevard for the exterior of a funeral home in 'Smart-Aleck Kill' and the exterior of the police station on Georgia Street for various episodes.

Other Los Angeles locations for the television series range from Beverly Hills to Hollywood, from Pasadena to Santa Monica. Around the area of Westwood village (which includes the University of California at Los Angeles (UCLA) and which houses a great collection of Chandleriana, manuscripts, notebooks, memorabilia) there are many streets and houses which retain their thirties look when Chandler wrote, in 'Blackmailers Don't Shoot': 'The apartment house stood on a hill above Westwood Village and was new and rather cheap looking.' That 'new' apartment house, if it survives, is doubtless one of the

*See above, p. 87.

Huge new skyscrapers now dominate the Bunker Hill area described in 'The King in Yellow'

*Westwood is described in Chandler's very first story, 'Blackmailers Don't Shoot'.
It was one of the first 'village' suburbs to be developed in the early twenties, and
architectural remnants of the thirties – like this bank and cinema – can still be
seen amidst the many new high-rise buildings*

Chandler himself lived and wrote for a time in the attractive, leafy suburb of Brentwood, mentioned in the early short stories. Carole Lombard also lived there, Marilyn Monroe ended her life there and some of today's film and television celebrities live in houses like these

charming period pieces that make the district such an expensive residential area.

Chandler himself lived for a short time in adjoining Brentwood, although, ever restless – he is reputed to have lived in over seventy locations in and around Los Angeles – he does not seem to have given it the benefit of one of his sharply observed descriptions. Brentwood's other claim to fame – if that is the word – which Chandler would have noted had he lived, is that it contains the modest little house in which Marilyn Monroe was discovered dead from an overdose of drugs. Otherwise its quiet, shady streets, its neat villas with their manicured lawns, provide a happy hunting ground for film and television directors looking for period locations, not least Carole Lombard's lovely Art-

Deco villa with its curving walls and porthole windows, which still remains intact. Farther west, near the coast, is Pacific Palisades, another area where Chandler lived and which has homes ranging from the ubiquitous wood-frame bungalows to the big ranch-style villas built in the thirties for film stars and rich business tycoons.

But every area described in the short stories, just as in the novels, from 'Bay City' in the extreme west to Pasadena in the north, from Hollywood and Beverly Hills in the centre to the City of Los Angeles in the east, presents a topographical treasure hunt as absorbing to twentieth-century explorers of their own times as was Schliemann's nineteenth-century quest for Troy. The television series brings the whole Chandler/Marlowe setting neatly full circle with the use of one particular location: right in the heart of Hollywood is High Tower Drive, a cul-de-sac at the end of which there is a tall lift-shaft tower flanked on each side with two perfectly preserved Art-Deco apartment

Small wood-frame bungalows in Bronson Canyon, Hollywood, one of which is used for Ann Riordan's house in the television series 'Philip Marlowe, Private Eye'. From 'Marlowe, Private Eye', a David Wicks television production

Despite the period cars, this photograph of Pasadena City Hall was taken in 1983 while shooting the episode 'Finger Man' for the television series. From 'Marlowe, Private Eye', a David Wicks television production

Hightower, Broadview Terrace, Hollywood, used by Chandler himself in Farewell, My Lovely, *by Robert Altman in* The Long Goodbye *and by producer David Wicks for 'The King in Yellow' episode of the television series 'Philip Marlowe, Private Eye'. From 'Marlowe, Private Eye', a David Wicks television production*

houses. Chandler himself used this setting as Sternwood Heights, home of the very sinister Jules Amthor, 'Psychic Consultant', in *Farewell, My Lovely*; Robert Altman used those self-same buildings as Marlowe's scruffy apartment in the film *The Long Goodbye*; for television David Wicks uses them as the location for the murder of Dolores Chiozza's maid in 'The King in Yellow'. The television series serves – ironically perhaps, for television effectively killed off the movies as the supreme entertainment medium for the masses – as the apotheosis to Chandler's Los Angeles.

The thirties and forties, when Chandler was creating his best-known works, was the heyday of Hollywood, the golden age of the big studios and the big stars. Hollywood recorded and romanticized, distorted and developed every aspect of American – and world – history; yet no American folk hero, even the cowboy, owes his existence so much to one man, Chandler, and the mediums he served, as does the private eye. He is not just the typical American hero but, more specifically, a Hollywood hero; and Marlowe is the supreme example. Now he is enshrined in a series which, like Chandler's own work, also catches the look, the atmosphere, the style of Los Angeles in what was arguably its greatest epoch.